Bertrand Russell

Has Man a Future?

'*Accurst be he that first invented war*'
MARLOWE

PENGUIN BOOKS

Penguin Books Ltd, Harmondsworth, Middlesex, England
Penguin Books, Inc., 3300 Clipper Mill Road
Baltimore 11, Md, U.S.A.
Penguin Books Pty Ltd
Ringwood, Victoria, Australia

First published 1961
simultaneously with a hard-cover edition by
Allen & Unwin
Reprinted 1962 (twice), 1964, 1965

Made and printed in Great Britain
by Hazell Watson & Viney Ltd
Aylesbury, Bucks
Set in Intertype Times

A PENGUIN SPECIAL

S 206

HAS MAN A FUTURE?

BERTRAND RUSSELL

By Bertrand Russell

THE A.B.C. OF RELATIVITY
THE ANALYSIS OF MATTER
HUMAN SOCIETY IN ETHICS AND POLITICS
THE IMPACT OF SCIENCE ON SOCIETY
NEW HOPES FOR A CHANGING WORLD
AUTHORITY AND THE INDIVIDUAL
HUMAN KNOWLEDGE: ITS SCOPE AND LIMITS
HISTORY OF WESTERN PHILOSOPHY
THE PRINCIPLES OF MATHEMATICS
INTRODUCTION TO MATHEMATICAL PHILOSOPHY
THE ANALYSIS OF MIND
OUR KNOWLEDGE OF THE EXTERNAL WORLD
AN OUTLINE OF PHILOSOPHY
THE PHILOSOPHY OF LEIBNIZ
AN INQUIRY INTO MEANING AND TRUTH
LOGIC AND KNOWLEDGE
THE PROBLEMS OF PHILOSOPHY
PRINCIPIA MATHEMATICA
FACT AND FICTION

MY PHILOSOPHICAL DEVELOPMENT
COMMON SENSE AND NUCLEAR WARFARE
WHY I AM NOT A CHRISTIAN
PORTRAITS FROM MEMORY
UNPOPULAR ESSAYS
POWER
IN PRAISE OF IDLENESS
THE CONQUEST OF HAPPINESS
SCEPTICAL ESSAYS
MYSTICISM AND LOGIC
THE SCIENTIFIC OUTLOOK
MARRIAGE AND MORALS
EDUCATION AND THE SOCIAL ORDER
ON EDUCATION

FREEDOM AND ORGANIZATION, 1814–1914
PRINCIPLES OF SOCIAL RECONSTRUCTION
ROADS TO FREEDOM
PRACTICE AND THEORY OF BOLSHEVISM
PROSPECTS OF INDUSTRIAL CIVILIZATION
(*In collaboration with Dora Russell*)

SATAN IN THE SUBURBS
NIGHTMARES OF EMINENT PERSONS

BERTRAND RUSSELL'S BEST
(*Edited by Robert E. Egner*)

THE BASIC WRITINGS OF BERTRAND RUSSELL
(*Edited by Lester E. Denonn and Robert E. Egner*)

Contents

1 *Prologue or Epilogue?** *

'MAN, or *homo sapiens,* as he somewhat arrogantly calls himself, is the most interesting, and also the most irritating, of animal species on the planet Earth.'

This might be the first sentence of the last chapter of a report on our flora and fauna by a philosophic Martian biologist. For us, deeply involved, as we all are, both emotionally and instinctively, it is difficult to achieve the impartiality and the breadth of outlook which would be natural to a visitor from another world. But it is useful, from time to time, to attempt such a contemplation as that of our supposed Martian, and in the light of this contemplation to assess the past, the present, and the future (if any) of our species, and the value, for good or evil, of what Man has done, is doing, and may do here- after, to life on earth, and perhaps in the future, to life elsewhere. In this kind of survey, temporary passions lose their importance, as small hills look flat from an aero- plane, whereas what is of permanent importance stands out more boldly than in a more restricted view.

Man, at first, seemed to have no very promising out- look in the general struggle for existence. He was still a rare species, less agile than the monkey in climbing trees to escape from wild beasts, almost destitute of natural protection against cold in the way of fur, hampered by his long infancy, and with difficulty securing food in competition with other species. His only initial advantage was his brain. Gradually, this one advantage proved

* Further treatment of a theme that I have dealt with under the same title in *Human Society in Ethics and Politics.*

cumulative, and transformed him from a hunted fugitive into the Lord of the Earth. The early steps in this process are pre-historic, and their order is conjectural. He learned to tame fire, which had presented dangers similar in kind, though less in degree, to those of the release of nuclear energy in our own day. Fire not only improved his food, but by being kept burning at the mouth of his cave insured his safety while he slept. He invented spears and bows and arrows. He dug concealed pits in which infuriated mammoths hopelessly struggled. He domesticated animals, and at the dawn of history discovered the uses of agriculture.

But above all his other gains there was one which was supreme: language. Spoken language, one must suppose, developed very slowly from purely animal cries. Written language, at first not a representative of speech, was an outcome of informative pictures gradually more and more stylized. The immense merit of language was that it made possible the transmission of experience. What had been learned in one generation could be passed on whole to the next. Instruction could in a large measure replace personal experience. Writing, even more than speech, made possible the creation of a storehouse of knowledge, and the supplementing of memory by means of records. It was this facility of preserving what individuals had found out that, more than anything else, made human progress possible. There had been a time when there were biological improvements in brain capacity, with corresponding advance in genetic capacity. But that time ceased some 500,000 years ago. Since that time, native intelligence has increased little, if at all, and human progress has depended upon acquired skills handed on by tradition and education. The foundations were laid in prehistoric ages, presumably without conscious purpose, but, once laid, they rendered possible a continually accelerating advance in knowledge and mastery. The advance in the last five centuries has been greater than that in all previous recorded history. One of the troubles of our age is that habits of thought cannot change as quickly as techniques, with the result that, as skill increases, wisdom fades.

From the long millennia during which human survival had remained doubtful, Man emerged with useful skills and with instincts and habits moulded by his past struggles. He still had non-human dangers to contend with, such as famines, inundations, and volcanic eruptions. What could, in early days, be done against famine is related in the Book of Genesis. Against inundations two methods were attempted: the Chinese, at the dawn of their history, built dykes along the Yellow River, while Western Asia, as appears in the story of Noah, thought that the best protection was a virtuous life. They held this view also as regards eruptions, and gave it literary expression in the account of the destruction of Sodom and Gomorrah. To this day, the two types of theory, Chinese and West-Asian, have persisted in uneasy antagonism, but with a gradually increasing prevalence of the Chinese point of view. Quite recent developments, however, have shown that a virtuous life (not quite in the traditional sense) is as necessary to survival as dykes.

As Man emerged from the perils of his non-human environment, he brought with him into his new world the instinctive and emotional make-up by means of which he had survived through previous ages. He had needed a great degree of toughness and a passionate determination to survive if possible. He had needed alert wariness, watchful fear, and, in crises, courage in the face of danger. What was he to do with this apparatus of habits and passions when the old perils had been overcome? He found a solution, but unfortunately not a very happy one. He turned the hostility and suspicion, which he had hitherto directed towards lions and tigers, upon his fellow-men – not all of them, since many of the skills by which he had survived required social cooperation, but only those outside the cooperating unit. In this way, through tribal cohesion and organized war, he reconciled, for many centuries, the need of social cooperation with the instinctive ferocity and suspicion which past struggles had bred in him. From the dawn of history to our own day, skill created by intelligence has continually changed the environment, while instinct and emotion have, in the main, persisted as they had been shaped to suit a wilder and more primitive world.

The turning of fear and suspicion from the non-human world to rival groups of men generated a new degree of gregariousness. Man is not as completely social as ants or bees, who apparently never have any impulse to behave in an anti-social manner. Men have not infrequently killed their kings, but bees do not assassinate their queens.* A foreign ant, intruding by accident into an alien nest, is instantly put to death, and no 'pacifist' protest ever occurs. Dissident minorities are unknown, and social cohesion invariably governs the behaviour of each individual. With human beings this is not the case. Primitive man probably knew no social group larger than the family. As a result of danger from human enemies – so one must suppose – the family became enlarged into the

---

* Except in accordance with the law of the hive; sporadic tyrannicide is unknown.

tribe, which had, or was reputed to have, a common ancestor. War produced combinations of tribes, and thence nations, empires, and alliances. The necessary social cohesion often broke down, but when it did, defeat followed. In consequence, partly by natural selection, partly by awareness of self-interest, men became increasingly capable of cooperating in large groups and exhibiting a gregariousness which their ancestors lacked.

The world in which we live has been shaped by some 6,000 years of organized warfare. As a rule, defeated populations were exterminated or greatly reduced in numbers. Success in war depended upon various factors; the most important were larger population, greater technical skill, more perfect social cohesion, and zeal. From a purely biological point of view, we may consider anything a progress which increases the number of human beings who can live in a given area. From this rather narrow standpoint, many wars must be regarded as fortunate. The Romans must have greatly increased the population of most parts of the Western Empire. Columbus and his successors made the Western hemisphere support numbers very many times as great as those of pre-Columbian Indians. In China and India it was central governments, established after ages of warfare, that made their vast numbers possible. But this has by no means always been the result of wars. The Mongols did irreparable damage in Persia, as did the Turks in the empire of the Caliphs. Ruins in North Africa, in regions now desert, bear eloquent witness to the harm that was done by the fall of Rome. The Taiping rebellion is estimated to have caused more deaths than the First World War. In all these cases, victory had gone to the less civilized side. In spite of these contrary examples, however, it is probable that, on the balance, wars in the past have done more to increase than to diminish the numbers of the human population of our planet.

There is, however, another point of view than that of biology. From the point of view of mere numbers, ants are many hundred times as successful as men. I have seen in Australia vast regions empty of human beings, but populated by innumerable hordes of termites, but we do not, on that account, consider termites superior to ourselves. Man has merits additional to those which have made him the most numerous of large mammals. These merits, which are distinctively human, may be collectively designated as cultural. They are characteristic rather of individuals than of societies, and involve matters quite distinct from social coherence and capacity for victory in war.

The division of mankind into competing and often hostile nations has had a disastrously distorting effect upon national estimates as to who deserves honour. We in Britain have devoted our most conspicuous public monuments to Nelson and Wellington, whom we honour for their skill in killing foreigners. Strange to say, foreigners do not feel the same admiration as we do for those Britons who show this kind of cleverness. If you were to ask any educated non-Briton what he considered the chief glories of Britain, he would be much more likely to mention Shakespeare, Newton, and Darwin than Nelson and Wellington. The slaughter of foreigners may perhaps sometimes have been necessary in the interests of the human race in general, but when justified was of the nature of police work, and often expressed only national pride and rapacity. It is not for its skill in homicide that the human race deserves respect. When, as in the Egyp-

tian Book of the Dead, the possibly last man comes
before the Judge of the Underworld, and pleads that the
extinction of his species is a matter for regret, what arguments will he be able to offer? I wish he could say that
human life has, in general, been happy. But hitherto, at
any rate since the invention of agriculture and social in-
equality and organized war, the majority of the human
race has lived a life of hardship, excessive toil, and
occasional tragic disaster. Perhaps this will no longer
be the case in the future, since a modicum of wisdom
could now make all human life joyous; but whether this
modicum will be forthcoming, who can tell? Meantime,
it will be something other than a history of general happiness that our last man will have to offer for the appro-
bation of Osiris.

If I were the pleader to Osiris for the continuation of
the human race, I should say: 'O just and inexorable
judge, the indictment of my species is all too well de-
served, and never more so than in the present day. But
we are not all guilty, and few of us are without better
potentialities than those that our circumstances have developed. Do not forget that we have but lately emerged
from a morass of ancient ignorance and age-long struggle
for existence. Most of what we know we have discovered
during the last twelve generations. Intoxicated by our
new power over nature, many of us have been misled into
the pursuit of power over other human beings. This is an
ignis fatuus, enticing us to return to the morass from
which we have been partially escaping. But this wayward
folly has not absorbed all our energies. What we have
come to know about the world in which we live, about
nebulae and atoms, the great and the small, is more than
would have seemed possible before our own day. You

may retort that knowledge is not good except in the hands of those who have enough wisdom to use it well. But this wisdom also exists, though as yet sporadically and without the power to control events. Sages and prophets have preached the folly of strife, and if we listen to them we shall emerge into new happiness.

'It is not only what to avoid that great men have shown us. They have shown us also that it is within human power to create a world of shining beauty and transcendent glory. Consider the poets, the composers, the painters, the men whose inward vision has been shown to the world in edifices of majestic splendour. All this country of the imagination might be ours. And human relations, also, could have the beauty of lyric poetry. At moments, in the love of man and woman, something of this possibility is experienced by many. But there is no reason why it should be confined within narrow boundaries; it could, as in the Choral Symphony, embrace the whole world. These are things which lie within human power, and which, given time, future ages may achieve. For such reasons, Lord Osiris, we beseech Thee to grant us a respite, and a chance to emerge from ancient folly into a world of light and love and loveliness.'

Perhaps our prayer will be heard. In any case, it is because of such possibilities, which, so far as we know, exist only for Man, that our species is worth preserving.

2 *The Atom Bomb*

THE nuclear age in which the human race is living, and may soon be dying, began for the general public with the dropping of an atom bomb on Hiroshima on 6 August 1945. But for nuclear scientists and for certain American authorities, it had been known for some time that such a weapon was possible. Work towards making it had been begun by the United States, Canada, and Britain very soon after the beginning of the Second World War The existence of possibly explosive forces in the nucleus of atoms had been known ever since the structure of atoms was discovered by Rutherford. An atom consists of a tiny core called the 'nucleus' with attendant electrons circling round it. The hydrogen atom, which is the simplest and lightest, has only one electron. Heavier atoms have more and more as they go up the scale. The first discovery that had to do with what goes on in nuclei was radio-activity, which is caused by particles being shot out of the nucleus. It was known that a great deal of energy is locked up in the nucleus, but, until just before the outbreak of the Second World War, there was no way of releasing this energy in any large quantity. A revolutionary discovery was that, in certain circumstances, mass can be transformed into energy in accordance with Einstein's formula which stated that the energy generated is equal to the mass lost multiplied by the square of the velocity of light. The simplest illustration is in the relation of hydrogen and helium. A helium atom consists of four hydrogen atoms, and one might, therefore, have expected that it would have four times the mass of an hydrogen atom.

But this is not the case. Taking the mass of a helium atom as 4, the mass of the hydrogen atom is not 1, but 1·008. When four hydrogen atoms combine to make a helium atom, the excess is released as energy and ceases to exist as mass. That is why the sun is hot, because the sun is a helium factory. The same sort of thing happens whenever lighter elements combine to form heavier ones, and it is this process, called 'fusion', which is used in the H-bomb.

The A-bomb, however, used a different process, depending upon radio-activity. In this process, called 'fission', a heavier atom splits into two lighter atoms. In general, in radio-active substances this fission proceeds at a constant rate which is slow where substances occurring in nature are concerned. But there is one form of uranium called 'U235' which, when it is pure, sets up a chain reaction which spreads like fire, though with enormously greater rapidity. It is this substance which was used in making the atom bomb. There were a number of difficulties to be overcome. The first of these was to separate out U235 from ordinary uranium, of which it formed only a small portion. The traitor Fuchs did valuable work in furthering this process, and it is an ironic fact that if his treachery had been discovered sooner the A-bomb would not have been ready in time for use against the Japanese.

The fact that such a bomb should be possible had been evident to nuclear physicists since the chain reaction was discovered just before the beginning of the Second World War. In spite of all attempts at secrecy, many people knew that work towards its manufacture was in progress.

The political background of the atomic scientists' work

was the determination to defeat the Nazis. It was held –
I think rightly – that a Nazi victory would be an appalling
disaster. It was also held, in Western countries, that German scientists must be well advanced towards making an
A-bomb, and that if they succeeded before the West did
they would probably win the war. When the war was
over, it was discovered, to the complete astonishment of
both American and British scientists, that the Germans
were nowhere near success, and, as everybody knows, the
Germans were defeated before any nuclear weapons had
been made. But I do not think that nuclear scientists of
the West can be blamed for thinking the work urgent and
necessary. Even Einstein favoured it. When, however, the
German war was finished, the great majority of those
scientists who had collaborated towards making the A-
bomb considered that it should not be used against the
Japanese, who were already on the verge of defeat and,
in any case, did not constitute such a menace to the
world as Hitler. Many of them made urgent representa-
tions to the American Government advocating that, instead of using the bomb as a weapon of war, they should,
after a public announcement, explode it in a desert, and
that future control of nuclear energy should be placed in
the hands of an international authority. Seven of the
most eminent of nuclear scientists drew up what is known
as 'The Franck Report' which they presented to the
Secretary of War in June 1945. This is a very admirable
and far-seeing document, and if it had won the assent of
politicans none of our subsequent terrors would have
arisen. It points out that 'the success which we have
achieved in the development of nuclear power is fraught
with infinitely greater dangers than were all the inven-
tions of the past'. It goes on to point out that there is no

secret which can be kept for any length of time, and that
Russia will certainly be able to make an A-bomb within
a few years. It took Russia, in fact, almost exactly four
years after Hiroshima. The danger of an arms race is
stated in terms which subsequent years have horrifyingly
verified. 'If no efficient international agreement is
achieved,' it states, 'the race for nuclear armaments will
be on in earnest not later than the morning after our
first demonstration of the existence of nuclear weapons.
After this, it might take other nations three or four years
to overcome our present head start.' It proceeds to suggest methods of international control and concludes: 'If
the United States were to be the first to release this new
means of indiscriminate destruction upon mankind, she
would sacrifice public support throughout the world,
precipitate the race for armaments, and prejudice the
possibility of reaching an international agreement on the
future control of such weapons.' This was not an isolated
expression of opinion. It was a majority opinion among
those who had worked to create the bomb. Niels Bohr –
after Einstein, the most eminent of physicists at that time
– approached both Churchill and Roosevelt with earnest
appeals in the same sense, but neither paid any attention.
When Roosevelt died, Bohr's appeal lay unopened on his
desk. The scientists were hampered by the fact that they
were supposed to be unworldly men, out of touch with
reality, and incapable of realistic judgements as to policy.
Subsequent experience, however, has confirmed all that
they said and has shown that it was they, and not the
generals and politicians, who had insight into what was
needed.

Indignant atomic scientists, after Hiroshima, inaugurated a monthly review, *The Bulletin of the Atomic Scien-*

tists, which has continued ever since to present the sane view on atomic weapons and atomic warfare.

I expressed a view which was substantially the same as that of The Franck Report, which I had not then seen, in a speech in the House of Lords on 28 November 1945. I said, and I quote the speech in full since it has appeared only in the proceedings of the House of Lords: *

My Lords, it is with very great diffidence that I rise to address you, both because I have only once before addressed your Lordships' House and because, after listening to the debate yesterday and today, I feel that other speakers have ten times the political knowledge and twenty times the experience that has fallen to my lot, and that it is an impertinence for me to say anything at all. At the same time, the subject to which I wish to confine my remarks – namely, the atomic bomb and its bearing on policy – is so important and weighs so heavily upon my mind that I feel almost bound to say something about what it means for the future of mankind.

I should like to begin with just a few technical points which I think are familiar to everybody. The first is that the atomic bomb is, of course, in its infancy, and is quite certain very quickly to become both much more destructive and very much cheaper to produce. Both those points I think we may take as certain. Then there is another point which was raised by Professor Oliphant, and that is that it will be not very difficult to spray a countryside with radio-active products which will kill every living thing throughout a wide area, not only human beings but every insect, every sort of thing that lives. And there is a further point which perhaps relates to the somewhat more distant future. As your Lordships know, there are in theory two ways of tapping nuclear

* *Hansard*, Official Report, House of Lords, Vol. 138, No. 30. Wednesday, 28 November 1945.

energy. One is the way which has now been made practicable, by breaking up a heavy nucleus into nuclei of medium weight. The other is the way which has not yet been made practicable, but which, I think, will be in time, namely, the synthesizing of hydrogen atoms to make heavier atoms, helium atoms or perhaps, in the first instance, nitrogen atoms. In the course of that synthesis, if it can be effected, there will be a very much greater release of energy than there is in the disintegration of uranium atoms. At present this process has never been observed but it is held that it occurs in the sun and in the interior of other stars. It only occurs in nature at temperatures comparable to those you get in the inside of the sun. The present atomic bomb in exploding produces temperatures which are thought to be about those in the inside of the sun. It is therefore possible that some mechanism analogous to the present atomic bomb, could be used to set off this much more violent explosion which would be obtained if one could synthesize heavier elements out of hydrogen.

All that must take place if our scientific civilization goes on, if it does not bring itself to destruction; all that is bound to happen. We do not want to look at this thing simply from the point of view of the next few years; we want to look at it from the point of view of the future of mankind. The question is a simple one: Is it possible for a scientific society to continue to exist, or must such a society inevitably bring itself to destruction? It is a simple question but a very vital one. I do not think it is possible to exaggerate the gravity of the possibilities of evil that lie in the utilization of atomic energy. As I go about the streets and see St Paul's, the British Museum, the Houses of Parliament, and the other monuments of our civilization, in my mind's eye I see a nightmare vision of those buildings as heaps of rubble with corpses all round them. That is a thing we have got to face, not only in our own country and cities, but throughout the civilized world as a real probability unless the world will agree to find a way of abolishing war. It is not enough to make war rare; great and serious war has got to be abolished, because otherwise these things will happen.

To abolish war is, of course, a very difficult problem. I have no desire to find fault with those who are trying to tackle that problem; I am quite sure I could not do any better. I simply feel that this is a problem that man has got to solve; otherwise man will drop out and the planet will perhaps be happier without us, although we cannot be expected to share that view. I think we have got to find a way of dealing with this. As everybody is aware, the immediate difficulty is to find a way of cooperating with Russia in dealing with it. I think that what the Prime Minister achieved in Washington was probably as much as could, at that time, be achieved. I do not suppose he could have done any better at that time. I am not one of those who favour the unconditional and immediate revelation to Russia of the exact processes by which the bomb is manufactured. I think it is right that conditions should be attached to that revelation, but I make the proviso that the conditions must be solely those which will facilitate international cooperation; they must have no national object of any sort or kind. Neither we nor America must seek any advantage for ourselves, but if we are to give the secret to the Russians, it must be on the basis that they are willing to cooperate.

On that basis, I think, it would be right to let them know all about it as soon as possible, partly, of course, on the grounds that the secret is a short term one. Within a few years the Russians will no doubt have bombs every bit as good as those which are at present being made in the United States; so it is only a question of a very short time during which we have this bargaining point, if it is one. The men of science, as your Lordships know, who have been concerned with the work are all extremely anxious to have the process revealed at once. I do not altogether agree with that, for the reasons I have stated, but I think it can be used as a means of getting a more sincere and a more thorough-going cooperation between ourselves and Russia. I find myself a whole-hearted supporter of the Foreign Secretary in the speeches he has made. I do not believe that the way to secure Russian cooperation is merely to express a desire for it. I think it is absolutely necessary to be firm on what we consider to be vital interests. I think it is more likely that you will get genuine cooperation from a certain firmness rather than merely going to them and begging them to co-operate. I agree entirely with the tone the Foreign Secretary has adopted on those matters.

We must, I think, hope – and I do not think this is a chimerical hope – that the Russian Government can be made to see that the utilization of this means of warfare would mean destruction to themselves as well as to every-body else. We must hope that they can be made to see that this is a universal human interest and not one on which countries are divided. I cannot really doubt that if that were put to them in a convincing manner they would see it. It is not a very difficult thing to see, and I cannot help thinking that they have enough intelligence to see it, provided it is separated from politics and from competition. There is, as everybody repeats, an attitude of suspicion. That attitude of suspicion can only be got over by complete and utter frank-ness, by stating 'There are these things which we consider vital, but on other points we are quite willing that you should stand up for the things you consider vital. If there is any point which we both consider vital, let us try to find a compromise rather than that each side should annihilate the other, which would not be for the good of anybody.' I cannot help thinking that if that were put in a perfectly frank and unpolitical manner to the Russians they would be as capable of seeing it as we are – at least I hope so.

I think one could make some use of the scientists in this matter. They themselves are extremely uneasy, with a very bad conscience about what they have done. They know they had to do it but they do not like it. They would be very thankful if some task could be assigned to them which would somewhat mitigate the disaster that threatens mankind. I think they might be perhaps better able to persuade the Russians than those of us who are more in the game; they could, at any rate, confer with Russian scientists and perhaps get an entry that way towards genuine cooperation. We have, I think, some time ahead of us. The world at the moment is in a war-weary mood, and I do not think it is unduly optimistic to suppose there will not be a great war within the next ten years. Therefore we have some time during which we can generate the necessary genuine mutual understanding.

There is one difficulty that I think is not always sufficiently understood on our side, and that is that the Russians always feel – and feel, as it appears, rightly – that in any conflict of interests there will be Russians on one side and everybody else on the other. They felt that over the Big Three versus the Big Five question; it was Russia on one side and either two or four on the other. When people have that feeling, you have, I suppose, to be somewhat tender in bargaining with them and certainly not expect them to submit to a majority. You cannot expect that, when they feel that it is themselves against the field. There will no doubt have to be a good deal of tact employed during the coming years to bring about continuing international cooperation.

I do not see any alternative to the proposal which is before the world of making the United Nations the repository. I do not think that there is very much hope in that, because the United Nations, at any rate at present, are not a strong military body, capable of waging war against a great Power; and whoever is ultimately to be the possessor of the atomic bomb will have to be strong enough to fight a great Power. Until you can create an international organization of that sort, you will not be secure. I do not think that there is any use whatever in paper prohibitions, either of the use or of the manufacture of bombs, because you cannot enforce them, and the penalty for obeying such a prohibition is greater than the penalty for infringing it, if you are really thinking of war. I do not think, therefore, that these paper arrangements have any force in them at all.

You have first to create the will to have international. control over this weapon, and, when that exists, it will be easy to manufacture the machinery. Moreover, once that machinery exists, once you have an international body which is strong and which is the sole repository of the use of atomic energy, that will be a self-perpetuating system. It will really prevent great wars. Habits of political action will grow up about it, and we may seriously hope that war will disappear from the world. That is, of course, a very large order; but this is what we all have to face: either war stops or else the whole of civilized mankind stops, and you are left with mere remnants, a few people in outlying districts, too unscientific to manufacture these instruments of destruction. The only people who will be too unscientific to do that will be people who have lost all the traditions of civilization; and that is a disaster so grave that I think that all the civilized nations of the world ought to realize it. I think they probably can be brought to realize it before it is too late. At any rate I most profoundly hope so.

At that time, when opinion had not hardened, the House of Lords listened to me with approval and, so far as I could judge, this approval was equal in all parties. Unfortunately, subsequent events put an end to this un-animity. But, for my part, I see nothing to withdraw in what I then said.

The United States Government, although it could not deny itself the pleasure of exhibiting its new powers of wholesale slaughter, did attempt, after the Japanese surrender, to give effect to some of the ideas which the atomic scientists had suggested. In 1946, it presented to the world what is called 'The Baruch Plan', which had very great merits and showed considerable generosity, when it is remembered that America still had an unbroken nuclear monopoly. The Baruch Plan proposed an International Atomic Development Authority which was to have a monopoly of mining uranium and thorium, refining the ores, owning materials, and constructing and operating plants necessary for the use of nuclear power. It was suggested that this Authority should be established by the United Nations and that the United States should give it the information of which, so far, America was the sole possessor. Unfortunately, there were features of the Baruch proposal which Russia found unacceptable, as, indeed, was to be expected. It was Stalin's Russia, flushed with pride in the victory over the Germans, suspicious (not without reason) of the Western Powers, and aware that in the United Nations it could almost always be outvoted. The creation of a World Authority, which is an obvious necessity if the danger of nuclear war is to be averted, has always been opposed by Russia as involving the stabilizing and perpetuating of economic and political systems which, according to the Communist creed, are evil. If Russia is to be brought to accept any kind of International Authority, it will have to be one which does not give a definite superiority to non-Communist Powers. This the Baruch Plan did not do. It could, perhaps, have been amended in a manner to obviate Russian objections, but the Soviet Government bluntly refused to discuss it or to entertain the possibility of anything of the kind. The consequence was a rapid worsening of relations between Russia and the West, and very soon American opinion became such that no similar propósal could again be made.

In spite of what scientists had told military men and politicians, both they and the American public continued to believe that America possessed a secret which could be kept from Russia for a long time, and that the exclusive possession of atomic weapons by the United States insured the safety of the West. When, in August 1949, it became known that Russia also had atomic weapons, it was supposed that this was due to spies and traitors, although, in fact, they probably accelerated the process very little. Unfortunately, the conviction that it was traitors, rather than Russian skill, which had deprived America of its monopoly, produced a general atmosphere of suspicion and gave rise to the reign of McCarthy and those who thought as he did. Neither in America, nor in Russia, nor yet in Britain or France, did statesmen or public opinion show any of that long-range wisdom which had inspired the best of the scientists. Hate was considered synonymous with patriotism, and preparations for war were thought to be the only safeguard of peace. The world was set upon a wrong course, and, in coming years, it travelled further and further along the road towards disaster.

3 *The H-Bomb*

THE A-bomb, when it was new, had caused a shudder of horror, and had even stimulated suggestions for international control of atomic energy. But people soon got used to it and came to realize that the harm which it could do was not enough to satisfy mutual ferocity. It was realized that, although the A-bomb could destroy cities, it could not exterminate sparse rural populations. Both sides, therefore, set to work frantically to invent something worse. The something worse that they invented was the H-bomb. It is by no means clear whether Russia or America was the winner of the race for this new weapon. In any case, the race was a very close one. The H-bomb is roughly a thousand times more powerful than the A-bomb. The explosion at Bikini has been variously estimated as generating energy equal to that generated by from fifteen to twenty-two million tons of TNT. Its capacity became known to the Western world by the Bikini test of the 1 March 1954. This test explosion surpassed all the expectations of Americans who had made it possible. It remains, as yet, the most deadly weapon possessed by either side.

'H-bomb' is really a misnomer, since the bulk of the explosive force is still derived from uranium. The explosion proceeds in three stages. One might compare it to lighting a fire which is made with paper and wood and coal: the wood is more difficult to light than the paper, and the coal is more difficult to light than the wood. In the H-bomb, there is first, as in the A-bomb, a supply of U235. The heat generated by the fission of U235 is sufficient to cause the fusion of a supply of hydrogen into helium. Both the U235 and the hydrogen are surrounded by a thick shell of ordinary uranium. The heat generated by the fusion of hydrogen into helium is sufficient to explode the ordinary uranium in the outer shell. Much the greater part of the energy released when an H-bomb explodes is due to its outer shell. The uranium atoms split into lighter atoms of many kinds, mostly radio-active. From the military point of view, the great advantage of the H-bomb comes from the employment of ordinary uranium, or, more exactly, from the employment of uranium from which the precious U235 has been extracted. It is only the immense heat which makes it possible to employ ordinary uranium in this way.

The harm done by the explosion of an H-bomb is not confined to the place where the explosion occurs. Radio-active products are hurled to a great height in the air, from which they are distributed all over the world and gradually descend, causing deadly diseases in man and poisoning water and vegetables and meat. The descent of these radio-active particles is called 'fall-out'. The radio-active substances that occur in fall-out are mostly such as do not occur in nature, or at any rate occur very rarely. The lethal properties of fall-out first became known to the public through an accident. A Japanese fishing vessel, which had the ironic name of 'Lucky Dragon', was well outside what American authorities had designated as the danger zone, but a sudden change of wind covered the ship with radio-active dust which caused all the sailors to become ill and one of them to die. Fall-out enormously increases the number of deaths to be expected from an H-bomb explosion.

What would happen in an H-bomb war is a matter of controversy. The United States Secretary of Defence, in 1958, summarizing a Pentagon report, estimated that, in a nuclear war between NATO and the Powers of the Warsaw Pact, 160 million Americans would die, 200 million Russians, and everybody in Western Europe and Britain. There were some who feared that such estimates might cool the ardour for NATO in Western Europe and Britain. Such, however, was not the case. Some strange and inexplicable death-wish seems to have spread over the Western world, and, so far, accounts of the horrors to be expected in a nuclear war have produced no action by Western Governments to prevent it, and have very little affected public opinion in the same direction. Lt-General James Gavin, at that time Chief of the U.S. Army Research and Development, was questioned before a U.S. Senate Sub-Committee in May 1956. Senator Duff asked him: 'If we got into nuclear war and our strategic air force made an assault in force against Russia with nuclear weapons so that those weapons were exploded in a way where the prevailing winds would carry them south-east over Russia, what would be the effect in the way of death over there under those circumstances, in your opinion?' General Gavin replied: 'I will give you an answer to this and I will give you a specific one, Sir, but I would like to respectfully suggest that the air force or a proper study group give you this answer. Current planning estimates run on the order of several hundred million deaths that would be either way depending upon which way the wind blew. If the wind blew to the south-east they would be mostly in the U.S.S.R., although they would extend into the Japanese and perhaps down into the Philippine area. If the wind blew the other way they would extend well back up into Western Europe.' *

It appeared from this statement that it depended upon the accident of the wind whether most of the casualties caused by an American attack upon Russia would be Russian or Western European. General Gavin's statement was too honest to suit the authorities, and he fell out of favour.

The question of survival in a nuclear war is a controversial one. Those who, like Herman Kahn, in his big book *On Thermonuclear War*, wish to encourage populations to risk the carnage, argue that, by means of enormous deep shelters, it would be possible to save a large part of the population. Kahn urges that the United States should spend thirty billion dollars on civil defence (p. 517), but he does not expect that this sum will, in fact, be spent, and his reasons for thinking that it would save many lives do not bear examination. I think the best that can reasonably be expected is said by John M. Fowler in *Fallout* (p. 175): 'A skilled and resourceful individual or family outside the ring of complete destruction and on the outskirts of the lethal umbrella of fallout might survive the nightmarish early weeks. By burrowing into the walls of the basement or huddling under some hastily improvised shield in a corner, a person might survive although the outdoors was an oven of silent death.' Even this, in view of the poisoning of food and water, the absence of all means of transport, the destruction of hospitals, and the paucity of surviving medical men, must be regarded as erring on the side of optimism. One must consider, not only the physical health of possible survivors after a nuclear war, but also what degree of mental

* *Bulletin of the Atomic Scientists*, No. 12, p. 270, 1956.

health could be expected after an emotional shock greater than any that any human being has hitherto endured. It is to be expected that many, if not most, of the survivors would have become insane and probably destructive. And it is not only actual nuclear warfare that presents this danger, but also the steps recommended by advocates of civil defence. Some, like Kahn, believe that a considerable proportion of Americans could be saved. I think this is an optimistic forecast. But even supposing it correct, what will be the mental condition of those who finally emerge into a dead and devastated world? Is it at all likely that any considerable percentage of them will be capable of the energetic work of reconstruction without which recovery will be impossible? What life in the shelters might be like has been vividly portrayed in a book that has not received the publicity which it deserves: *Level 7*, by Mordecai Roshwald.

There is, perhaps, one ray of hope; fall-out tends not to cross the Equator, and, if the war were mainly confined to the Northern Hemisphere, the empire of the world might be held by the present South African Government. This, no doubt, would be hailed as a victory of the 'FREE WORLD'.

Certain things have been obvious to everybody who has considered the dangers: one is the urgency of nuclear disarmament; a second is the importance of abandoning nuclear tests; a third is the danger inherent in the present policy of instant retaliation; a fourth is the prevention of the spread of nuclear weapons to Powers which do not yet possess them. Although the necessity for action about all these four matters is universally admitted, nothing has been achieved in regard to any of them. I will say something about each.

Disarmament conferences have been held with wearisome frequency. There is a constant technique at such conferences. Each side is anxious to claim that it favours peace, and each side, therefore, comes forward with a proposal which, if adopted, might have considerable merit, but each side takes care that its proposal should contain something that the other side is pretty sure to reject, and neither side is willing to seek a reasonable compromise, since that would be thought to be cowardly appeasement. Once, in 1955, the West had a nasty jolt in applying this technique. It made some excellent proposals for disarmament, but, to the horror of Western Governments, the U.S.S.R. accepted the proposals – whereupon the West immediately withdrew them. The details of this affair can be read in Philip Noel-Baker's book *The Arms Race*. I think that anyone who reads this book will be forced to the conclusion that neither East nor West genuinely desires disarmament and that each is only concerned to find ways of advocating it without getting it.

The abolition of nuclear tests has been the subject of long negotiations which have often looked as if they might succeed, but always one side or the other has introduced new contentious matter which made agreement difficult. It is still *possible* that agreement may be reached, but it cannot be said that the outlook is hopeful. The blame for failure falls mainly on the U.S.S.R.

The importance of abolishing tests is twofold: on the one hand, it would make the spread of nuclear weapons to new Powers more difficult and, on the other hand, it would put an end to the evils of fall-out so long as peace lasted. Fall-out is of various different kinds. Perhaps Strontium 90 and Carbon 14 are the most important. It consists of radio-active dust brought down from the upper atmosphere by rain or wind or merely by the slow operation of gravity. It causes various troubles. Bone cancer and leukemia and damage to the germ cells are the most serious. As these troubles occur in any case with a certain frequency, it is impossible to say in any given case that fall-out is the cause of the trouble. But everybody, except certain interested parties, is agreed that the tests which occurred up to 1958 increased the number of deaths from cancer and the number of births of defective children. Governments spend a certain amount of money on research for the prevention of cancer, but they spend an enormously larger amount on causing cancer. As for the genetic effects, I will quote the opinion of a distinguished American specialist in heredity, A. H. Sturtevant. He has stated: 'There is no possible escape from the conclusion that the bombs already exploded will ultimately result in the production of numerous defective individuals – if the human race itself survives for many generations. ... I regret that an official [Admiral Strauss] in a position of such responsibility should have stated that there is no biological hazard from low doses of high energy radiation.'

Not long afterwards the same scholar stated in a public address that probably 1,800 of the children born in 1954, the year of the test of the bomb, were already infected as a result of the high degree of radio-activity released. In the same year the American zoologist Curt Stern declared: 'By now everyone in the world harbours in his body small amounts of radio-activity from past H-bomb tests; "hot" strontium in bones and teeth, "hot" iodine in thyroid glands.' *

It is extraordinary, and very depressing, to observe

* *Brighter Than a Thousand Suns*, pp. 303–4.

how the arms race distorts the moral sense. If I deliberately caused cancer in one person, I should be considered a monster of iniquity, but, if I deliberately cause it to some thousands of people, I am a noble patriot.

The genetic damage has the horrible property of being hereditary. A person who has suffered such damage may, by luck, have healthy children, but they will carry the taint which may come out in their children. How many people have been genetically damaged by the tests that have already taken place, it is impossible to ascertain, and the estimates that have been published have varied according to the political opinions of those who made them, but it is practically certain that there has been genetic damage and that in a nuclear war such damage would be very widespread among such survivors as might remain. The vision of a sparsely populated world consisting of people only capable of generating idiots or monsters is to be commended to the consideration of those comfortable gentlemen who calmly contemplate the possibility of nuclear explosions.

The doctrine of instant retaliation, which has been explicitly advocated in the West and is probably also held in the East, is one for which from a military point of view there are strong arguments. It arises from the fact that an unexpected attack in the style of Pearl Harbor would give a great advantage to the side that made it, and, if the other side is not to be completely crippled, it must retaliate at once before it is irreparably damaged. Each side believes that the other *may*, at any moment, make an unprovoked attack, and each side, therefore, has to be in constant readiness to retort by a counterattack upon the aggressor. We know more about what is done in this respect by the West than by the East. The

United States has a vast circle of radar stations always on the look-out for any sign of the approach of any Soviet bombers or missiles. As soon as radar is thought to signal such an approach, American H-bombs start towards Russia. Frequently, mistakes are made. Sometimes flights of wild birds, and once, at least, the moon, have been mistaken for Russian missiles. The alert has been given, and the bombers have started on their way. Hitherto, the mistake has been discovered in time and the bombers have been recalled, but there is no security that future mistakes will be discovered before it is too late, and, if they are not, the world will be plunged into an unintended nuclear war. In any given month this is not very probable, but the probability increases with the time and, in the course of the months and years throughout which we are told to expect the cold war to continue, it becomes almost a certainty. So long as the doctrine of instant retaliation with H-bombs continues to be in force, it is only by luck that we survive throughout the present or any future year. This is one of the most urgent reasons in favour of nuclear disarmament.

The spread of H-bombs to Powers which do not already possess them is obviously undesirable since it very much increases the likelihood of nuclear war. Although this is universally recognized, nothing effective is done about it. Originally, only the United States had nuclear weapons, then the u.s.s.r. had them, and then Great Britain. Now, France in all probability has them. It cannot be long before China has them. In the end, a very great many Powers will possess them. If nothing is done, the time is not far distant when any two minor Powers could embroil the whole world. But, although everybody knows this, nothing whatever is done.

So far, the H-bomb is the worst weapon of mass destruction that has been invented, but it is obvious that, if international anarchy and scientific skill both continue, even more dangerous weapons will be invented, probably quite soon. There has been talk of what is called 'The Doomsday Machine'. This would be a machine which could, in a moment, destroy the whole population of the world. Herman Kahn has stated that, if he thought it worth while, he could almost certainly invent such a machine, but as yet, fortunately, he does not think it desirable to do so. It is clear, however, that if it were known how to construct this machine, some nation of fanatics, faced with the prospect of defeat, would probably employ it. I do not doubt that Hitler, in his last days, would have preferred the end of man to the ignominy of surrender.

Apart from the Doomsday Machine, there are other probabilities which must be borne in mind. Chemical and bacteriological warfare is as yet considered not so effective as H-bombs, but all the great Powers are engaged in attempts to perfect it and may succeed before long. Another possibility which may be realized fairly soon is that of manned satellites containing H-bombs. Imagine a world in which the sky is darkened by flights of Russian and American satellites returning, say, once a day, and each capable of inflicting enormous slaughter. Would life be livable under such conditions? Would human nerves be capable of enduring them? Would not universal apprehension, in the end, make people prefer sudden disaster to a life of daily and hourly terror? I do not know what horrors may be in store for us, but no one can doubt that, unless something very radical is done, scientific man is a doomed species. In the world in which we are living, there is an active and dominant will towards death which has, so far, at every crisis, got the better of sanity. If we are to survive, this state of affairs must not continue. In the remainder of this volume, I shall try to suggest ways by which we may yet emerge.

4 *Liberty or Death?*

PATRICK HENRY, an American patriot who rose to eminence during the War of Independence, is now chiefly remembered for his exclamation: 'Give me Liberty, or give me Death.' In the mouths of fanatical anti-Communists, this has become a slogan purporting to mean that a world without human beings would be preferable to a Communist world. As Patrick Henry meant it, however, it had a quite different significance. He was advocating a just cause, and, owing to British hostility, the cause could not triumph without the loss of American lives. Consequently, his death might promote liberty. In such circumstances, it is right and proper that his slogan should be approved.

When, however, this same slogan is used to justify a nuclear war, the situation is very different. We do not know what would be the outcome of a nuclear war. It might be the end of the human species. It might be the survival of a few scattered bands of anarchic plunderers in a world that had lost all social cohesion. It might, in the most favourable circumstances imaginable, result in very tight governmental despotisms with rigid rationing of all the necessaries of life. Herman Kahn, who is concerned to justify nuclear war in certain circumstances, admits that, at the best, it would result in what he calls 'disaster socialism' (p. 438). The one thing in which it could not possibly result is ordered liberty such as Patrick Henry wanted and his modern admirers pretend to want.*

* It is somewhat ironic that those who are most apt to quote Patrick Henry on Liberty or Death regard anybody who appeals

To die for a cause is noble if the cause is good and your death promotes it. If it is practically certain that your death will not promote it, your action shows merely fanaticism. It is particularly obvious in the case of those who say explicitly that they would prefer the extinction of our species to a Communist victory, or, alternatively, to an anti-Communist victory. Assuming Communism to be as bad as its worst enemies assert, it would nevertheless be possible for improvement to occur in subsequent generations. Assuming anti-Communism to be as bad as the most excessive Stalinists think it, the same argument applies. There have been many dreadful tyrannies in past history, but, in time, they have been reformed or swept away. While men continue to exist, improvement is possible; but neither Communism nor anti-Communism can be built upon a world of corpses.

Those who talk about the 'free world' and are the most active in promoting hatred of Communism show, in a number of ways, that they are not quite sincere in their professed policy. The British Government has lately gone out of its way to show friendship to Portugal, although Portugal is engaged in a brutal suppression of the non-white population of Angola. Spain, under Franco, has nearly, if not quite, as little liberty as Russia under Khrushchev, yet the West befriends Spain in every possible way. The Anglo-French Suez expedition was not much less wicked in intention than the Russian suppression of the Hungarian rebellion, though it did infinitely less harm because it was unsuccessful. In Cuba,

to the First or Fifth Amendment of the Constitution, both of which were carried mainly by the efforts of Patrick Henry, as *ipso facto* a traitor.

Guatemala, and British Guiana, Western Powers have displayed their determination to thwart the wishes of the inhabitants, provided this was possible and was necessary in order to keep them in the Western camp. Membership of the Communist Party has recently been made criminal in the United States, except in the case of those who can prove that they did not know Communism to be subversive. All these are crimes against liberty. And the more tense the situation becomes, the more such crimes will be thought justified in the cause of liberty.

There is in the West much more regimentation and much more misleading propaganda by the Establishment than is generaly known. Nor is it admitted that all such restrictions diminish the difference between East and West, and make the claim of the West to be called 'The Free World' derisory.

Consider, for example, the question of American bases in Britain. How many people know that within each of them there is a hard kernel consisting of the airmen who can respond to an alert and are so highly trained that they can be in the air within a minute or two? This kernel is kept entirely isolated from the rest of the camp, which is not admitted to it. It has its own mess, dormitories, libraries, cinemas, etc., and there are armed guards to prevent other Americans in the base camp from having access to it. Every month or two, everybody in it, including the Commander, is flown back to America and replaced by a new group. The men in this inner kernel are allowed almost no contact with the other Americans in the base camp and no contact whatever with any of the inhabitants of the neighbourhood.

It seems clear that the whole purpose is to keep the British ignorant and to preserve, among the personnel of the kernel, that purely mechanical response to orders and propaganda for which the whole of their training is designed. Moreover, orders to this group do not come from the Commandant, but direct from Washington. To suppose that at a crisis the British Government can have any control over the orders sent from Washington is pure fantasy. It is obvious that at any moment orders might be sent from Washington which would lead to reprisals by the Soviet forces and to the extermination of the population of Britain within an hour.

An extraordinarily interesting case which illustrates the power of the Establishment, at any rate in America, is that of Claude Eatherly, who gave the signal for the dropping of the bomb at Hiroshima. His case also illustrates that in the modern world it often happens that only by breaking the law can a man escape from committing atrocious crimes. He was not told what the bomb would do and was utterly horrified when he discovered the consequences of his act. He devoted himself throughout many years to various kinds of civil disobedience with a view to calling attention to the atrocity of nuclear weapons and to expiating the sense of guilt which, if he did not act, would weigh him down. The authorities decided that he was to be considered mad, and a board of remarkably conformist psychiatrists endorsed that official view. Eatherly was repentant and certified; Truman was unrepentant and uncertified. I have seen a number of Eatherly's statements explaining his motives. These statements are entirely sane. But such is the power of mendacious publicity that almost everyone, including myself, believed that he had become a lunatic.

Quite recently, as a result of publicity about Eatherly's case, the Attorney General in Washington intervened, and Eatherly, who had been locked up in the maximum security ward for half a year, was transferred to a section of the hospital where he enjoyed unusual privileges and had been told that he would be released without any fresh hearing in the near future. He was not released, but for the moment has escaped.

Consider, again, the sort of thing that happens in an investigation by the House Committee on un-American Activities. If some middle-aged man, whom this Committee happens to dislike, comes before it, something of the following kind is apt to occur:

Question: 'Thirty years ago, when you were a student, did you know any Communists?'

Answer: 'Yes.'

Question: 'Will you give their names?'

Answer: 'No.' *

The unfortunate man who is being interrogated is then liable to be sent to gaol for contempt of Congress unless, on reflection, he decides to win the respect of the Committee by giving his friends away or, better still, by inventing false accusations against his friends. This procedure also is supposed to be justified in the sacred name of liberty.

I do not mean what I have been saying as a defence of the U.S.S.R. The U.S.S.R., especially in Hungary and Eastern Germany, has shown a horrifying contempt of and cruelty towards those whom it has been oppressing. And it has been no more free from hypocrisy than the

---

* There is an impression that this sort of thing ceased with the death of Senator McCarthy. This is not the case. The latest instance known to me occurred on 4 April 1961 when Pete Seeger, a folk singer, was sentenced to one year's imprisonment for just such an offence.

West: the Government of Eastern Germany, restored solely by Russian military power, is called 'The German *Democratic* Republic'. But the fact that the East has been guilty of crimes does not prove the innocence of the West. Self-righteousness is prevalent on both sides, and on both sides is equally odious.

One of the dreadful things about nuclear weapons is that, if they are employed on a large scale, they will do immense harm, not only to the belligerents, but also to neutrals. The neutrals have, therefore, the elementary right of self-preservation in trying to prevent a nuclear war. Whatever right a country may have to preserve its own form of government in the face of foreign opposition, it cannot, with any justice, claim the right to exterminate many millions in countries which wish to keep out of the quarrel. How can it be maintained that, because many of us dislike Communism, we have a right to inflict death on innumerable inhabitants of India and Africa who wish only to be let alone? Can it be maintained that this is democracy? Would not democracy demand that uncommitted nations should not be involved without their own consent?

Consider, for example, the problem of Berlin. I observe with dismay that both the U.S. and the U.S.S.R. have expressed their readiness for nuclear war rather than submit to a solution which they dislike. Such pronouncements, involving unimaginable horror for the whole world, are intolerable, and only seem justifiable as a result of mutual melodrama. The wickedness of the Kremlin or of Wall Street, as the case may be, is a fundamental dogma with fanatics on both sides, which blinds them to their common interest. In negotiations between East and West, both sides, if they were sane, would not

regard each other as the enemy, but would view the
H-bomb as the common enemy of both. Both East and
West have a common interest, which is to escape the
common destruction threatened by modern weapons.
Both sides are blinded to this common interest by mutual
hatred. In negotiations there is no genuine wish on either
side to reach agreement, but only to avoid any semblance
of a diplomatic victory by the other side.

Behind this mutual enmity, there lie certain human
passions, of which the chief are pride, suspicion, fear,
and love of power. Negotiators consider that they have
reason to feel pride when they resist even reasonable
concessions, and in this they are usually supported by the
public opinion of their own country. Suspicion – which
is by no means groundless while the present temper remains unchanged on both sides – makes each side view
what the other side says as probably containing some
trap enticing our innocent negotiators by the diabolical
cunning of the other side. Fear – which, again, is by no
means irrational under present circumstances – has the
effect, which fear often has, of producing irrational reactions that increase the danger that is feared. This is a
common phenomenon in private life, well-known to
psychiatrists. In a state of terror, most people do not
think sanely but react in an instinctively animal manner.
I once had a donkey which was kept in an outhouse.
The outhouse caught fire, and it required the utmost
efforts of several strong men to drag the donkey to safety.
Left to itself, it would have been immobilized by terror
and would have been burnt to death. The situation of
the Great Powers in the present day is closely similar.
This applies especially to the question of disarmament.
Each side is terrified of the nuclear weapons of the other

side, and seeks safety by increasing its own nuclear armaments. The other side naturally responds by a new increase on its side. In consequence, all the steps taken to diminish the nuclear peril, increase it.

Love of power is, perhaps, an even stronger motive than fear in enticing nations to pursue irrational policies. Although individual boastfulness is considered to be bad manners, national boastfulness is admired – at any rate, by the compatriots of those who practise it. Throughout history, great nations have been led to disaster by unwillingness to admit that their power had limits. World conquest has been a will-o'-the-wisp by which one nation after another has been led to its downfall. Hitler's Germany is the most recent example. Going backwards in time, we find many other examples, of which Napoleon, Genghis Khan, and Attila are the most noteworthy. Those who regard Genesis as authentic history, may take Cain as the first example: he may well have thought that, with Abel out of the way, he could rule over coming generations. When Khrushchev threatens to obliterate the West, and when Dulles said, 'We might win the hot war,' I am reminded of past examples of a similar folly.

And it is an utter folly, even from the narrowest point of view of self-interest. To spread ruin, misery, and death throughout one's own country as well as that of the enemy is the act of madmen. If East and West could cease their enmity, they could devote their scientific skill to their own welfare, to living without the burden of fear that only their own silliness has caused. For it is in the hearts of men that the evil lies. The vast instruments of terror that have been built up are external monuments to our own evil passions. Nothing in the non-human world

affords any ground for existing hostilities. The trouble
lies in the minds of men, and it is in enlightening the
minds of men that the cure must be sought.

There are those who say: 'War is part of human nature,
and human nature cannot be changed. If war means the
end of man, we must sigh and submit.' This is always said
by those whose sigh is hypocritical. It is undeniable that
there are men and nations to whom violence is attractive,
but it is not the case that anything in human nature makes
it impossible to restrain such men and nations. Individuals who have a taste for homicide are restrained by the
criminal law, and most of us do not find life intolerable
because we are not allowed to commit murders. The same
is true of nations, however disinclined war-mongers may
be to admit it. Sweden has never been at war since 1814.
None of the Swedes that I have known has shown any
sign of suffering from thwarted instinct for lack of war.
There are many forms of peaceful competition which are
not to be deplored, and, in these, men's combative instincts can find full satisfaction. Political contests in a
civilized country often raise just the kind of issues that
would lead to war if they were between different nations.
Democratic politicians grow accustomed to the limitations imposed by law. The same would be true in international affairs if there were political machinery for
settling disputes and if men had become accustomed to
respecting it. Not long ago, private disputes were often
settled by duels, and those who upheld duelling maintained that its abolition would be contrary to human
nature. They forgot, as present upholders of war forget,
that what is called 'human nature' is, in the main, the
result of custom and tradition and education, and, in
civilized men, only a very tiny fraction is due to primitive

instinct. If the world could live for a few generations
without war, war would come to seem as absurd as duelling has come to seem to us. No doubt there would still
be some homicidal maniacs, but they would no longer be
heads of Governments.

5 Scientists and the H-Bomb

THERE is an impression in a large part of the general public that scientists are morally to blame for the peril to which nuclear weapons expose the world. There are some scientists to whom a portion of this blame can be legitimately assigned. They are those who are employed by their Governments in the construction of nuclear weapons, or in research with a view to such construction. But a considerable majority among eminent scientists have done what they could to combat the nuclear danger. Politicians, Press, and public have prevented the efforts of scientists from being widely known. In this chapter, I propose to say something about the efforts that they have made.

When the American Government first proposed to set to work constructing the H-bomb, Oppenheimer, who had been the main agent in the construction of the A-bomb, opposed the new project. The Authorities were outraged and, by raking up some long-ago indiscretions of which they had always been aware, they secured in 1954 a decision that he was to be regarded as a 'security risk' – that is to say, that he was no longer to have access to any confidential information.

There are those who may think that there was an inconsistency in being willing to make the A-bomb, but unwilling to make the H-bomb. The A-bomb was made in time of war when it was supposed (mistakenly, though with good reason) that Hitler was on the verge of discovering how to make it. The making of the H-bomb was undertaken in time of peace, when it was certain that, if the project were proceeded with, the U.S.S.R. would have it about as soon as the U.S., and it could not be a means of victory to either side.

Meanwhile, the proved destructiveness of the H-bomb had aroused the utmost alarm among practically all scientists who were not in the employment of their respective Governments. By the initiative of Count Bernadotte, a number of very eminent men of science (confined, however, to Western nations) met in the island of Mainau, and, on the 15 July 1955, they signed the following statement:

We who sign this appeal are scientists from many countries, of various races, different creeds, and different political convictions. But we all share the privilege of having been awarded the Nobel Prize.

We have been happy to devote a lifetime to the service of Science, for we think that Science is a way to a fuller life for mankind. But we are alarmed when realizing that it is this very Science which now provides man with the means of self-destruction.

By total war and the use of now available weapons the world may become so infested with radio-activity that war would result in the destruction of whole nations, annihilating both neutrals and belligerents.

Should the Big Powers engage in war, who can guarantee that it will not develop into such a deadly struggle? Thus any nation engaging in total war invites its own destruction and endangers the whole world.

We do not deny it is the fear of these destructive weapons by which Peace is maintained at present in this world. Yet we think it extremely deceptive for any Government to believe that fear of such weapons will, in the long run, prevent wars. On the contrary, fear and tensions have only too often led to the outbreak of wars. Likewise it also seems to us self-deception to imagine that minor conflicts could still be settled by employing the traditional weapons. No warring nation will, in times of extreme danger, deny itself the use of any weapons that scientific techniques can supply.

Thus all nations must arrive at the decision voluntarily to renounce force as the last recourse in foreign policy. For they will cease to exist if they are not prepared to do so.

Dr Linus Pauling, who has been one of the most active among scientists in the search for ways of diminishing the danger of nuclear war, drafted a petition to the United Nations urging an agreement to stop the tests as a first step towards the abolition of nuclear weapons. For this draft he received 9,235 signatures of scientists, and, in January 1958, he presented it to Mr Hammarskjöld. This influential petition said:

We, the scientists whose names are signed below, urge that an international agreement to stop the testing of nuclear bombs be made now.

Each nuclear bomb test spreads an added burden of radio-active elements over every part of the world. Each added amount of radiation causes damage to the health of human beings all over the world and causes damage to the pool of human germ plasm such as to lead to an increase in the number of seriously defective children that will be born in future generations.

So long as these weapons are in the hands of only three powers an agreement for their control is feasible. If testing continues, and the possession of these weapons spreads to additional Government, the danger of outbreak of a cataclysmic nuclear war through the reckless action of some irresponsible national leader will be greatly increased.

An international agreement to stop the testing of nuclear bombs now could serve as a first step toward a more general disarmament and the ultimate effective abolition of nuclear weapons, averting the possibility of a nuclear war that would be a catastrophe to all humanity.

We have in common with our fellow men a deep concern for the welfare of all human beings. As scientists we have knowledge of the dangers involved and therefore a special responsibility to make those dangers known. We deem it imperative that immediate action be taken to effect an international agreement to stop the testing of all nuclear weapons.

The Indian Government drew up a report written by thoroughly competent men of science, entitled 'Nuclear Explosions and their Effects'. This was published in Delhi in 1956; the second edition in 1958. It is admirably objective and reliable, but, for this reason, it did not serve the purposes of the politicians of East or West and offered nothing of interest to sensational journalists. Consequently, it was little known either in the East or in the West.

In August 1955, there was an important meeting in London of the Parliamentary Association for World Government at which there were four representatives from the U.S.S.R., and representatives from all other independent countries. The participants were by no means confined to members of Parliaments. There were scientists and sociologists and philosophers, and the organization and the agenda were largely arranged by scientists. The Russians, like the other participants, came in a completely friendly spirit and were welcomed with equal friendliness by the Western participants. It became obvious, as discussion proceeded, that, if the affairs of the world had been entrusted to such a body, the East-West tension could have been quickly lessened and many problems

which Governments have found insoluble could have
been settled in a manner involving no surrender of vital
interests by any party. At the beginning of the discussion, I moved a resolution:

Since in any future world war nuclear weapons will certainly be employed and since such weapons threaten the
continued existence of civilized life and possibly even of
mankind, we urge the Governments of the world to realize,
and to acknowledge publicly, that their purposes cannot be
furthered by world war: consequently we urge the immediate examination of the implications of recent scientific
developments for humanity as a whole and the promotion
of peaceful means for the settlement of all matters of international dispute.

At the end of the discussion, the following resolution
was carried unanimously:

Since the danger now exists that in case of any future
world war nuclear weapons may be used and since such
weapons threaten to cause immeasurable suffering and
destruction, we urge the Governments of the world to realize,
and to acknowledge publicly, that their purposes cannot be
furthered by world war: consequently we urge the immediate examination of the implications of recent scientific
developments for humanity as a whole and the promotion
of peaceful means for the settlement of all matters of international dispute.

To this I added:

The resolution as you may have observed is not exactly
as that I moved at the beginning of the conference. The
differences that exist are due to discussions with our friends,
the Soviet scientists, with whom I am happy to say we
arrived, after a very friendly discussion, at complete agreement at a resolution we could all manifestly support. That

agreement and unanimity is a very important thing. I am very glad indeed that the resolution has been able to be so drafted that it can be supported by our Soviet friends just as much as those in the West. It is a beginning to a cooperation which I hope will widen and deepen throughout the years until the divisions that have existed have passed away.

Professor C. A. Golounsky, of the Moscow Academy of Sciences, also spoke:

The Soviet scientists have entrusted me with the pleasant duty of telling you that they support the resolution. I want also especially to note the spirit of cooperation and mutual understanding in the steering committee which made it possible to arrive at unanimous approval of the resolution. The decisions of this Conference have no legal force. Their significance is exclusively of a moral character. But more important would be the fact of this resolution being adopted not by the majority but unanimously, expressing the feelings of everyone present here. We are sure that the adoption of this resolution will be a substantial contribution to the strengthening of international peace and the security of the peoples of the world.

Professor A. V. Topchiev, Scientific Secretary of the Soviet Academy, spoke in conclusion, saying, among other things:

The Soviet scientists think it our pleasant duty to point out that the Conference is definitely a success. The whole Conference worked in a spirit of mutual understanding and a sincere desire to come to an agreement. It is characteristic and significant that both the main resolution of the Conference and the decisions of the Commissions have been adopted unanimously. ... Our Conference has shown that any question can be agreed upon if all the participants sincerely desire to come to an agreement and show understanding to take into consideration the viewpoints of their partners. ... It is important to point out another positive feature of our Conference, and that is the meeting of scientists of different countries and personal contacts between them which will no doubt contribute both to the development and strengthening of international ties and to further successes of science.

The proceedings ended in an atmosphere of cordiality and of immense enthusiasm. The first two-thirds of the year 1955 was a period of hope. There was a large and very successful conference at Helsinki in June called 'The World Assembly for Peace' sponsored chiefly by Communists, but contributed to by non-Communists as well. I, myself, was not able to attend it, but sent a paper containing possible terms for settling East–West disputes which won approval from almost everybody at the conference. The hopeful atmosphere of that time was, however, destroyed by the Western Governments, which, when their proposals for disarmament were unexpectedly accepted by the U.S.S.R., immediately withdrew them. In recent months the same method has been employed by the U.S.S.R. to prevent the conclusion of the treaty banning nuclear tests.

The organization with which I myself was most closely connected was that which came to be known by the name of 'The Pugwash Movement'. This arose out of a statement which I sent in draft to a small number of men of science of the highest eminence, beginning with Einstein, who signed it two days before his death. My purpose was to secure cooperation between Communist and anti-Communist scientists on matters lying within their technical competence, and, if possible, also on international measures related to nuclear weapons. I thought that a statement signed by some twelve of the ablest men living at that time would, perhaps, have some effect upon Government and the public. When I had secured what seemed to me enough signatures for a beginning, I published the statement at a Press Conference, organized by a member of the staff of the *Observer* with very substantial assistance from the newspaper, on 9 July 1955, at which I had the great good fortune to have Professor Rotblat as Chairman. The text of this statement is as follows:

In the tragic situation which confronts humanity, we feel that scientists should assemble in conference to appraise the perils that have arisen as a result of the development of weapons of mass destruction, and to discuss a resolution in the spirit of the appended draft.

We are speaking on this occasion, not as members of this or that nation, continent, or creed, but as human beings, members of the species Man, whose continued existence is in doubt. The world is full of conflicts; and, over-shadowing all minor conflicts, the titanic struggle between Communism and anti-Communism.

Almost everybody who is politically conscious has strong feelings about one or more of these issues; but we want you, if you can, to set aside such feelings and consider yourselves only as members of a biological species which has had a remarkable history, and whose disappearance none of us can desire.

We shall try to say no single word which should appeal to one group rather than to another. All, equally, are in peril, and, if the peril is understood, there is hope that they may collectively avert it.

We have to learn to think in a new way. We have to learn to ask ourselves, not what steps can be taken to give military victory to whatever group we prefer, for there no longer are such steps; the question we have to ask ourselves is: what steps can be taken to prevent a military contest of which the issue must be disastrous to all parties?

The general public, and even many men in positions of authority, have not realized what would be involved in a war with nuclear bombs. The general public still thinks in terms of the obliteration of cities. It is understood that the new bombs are more powerful than the old, and that, while one A-bomb could obliterate Hiroshima, one H-bomb could obliterate the largest cities, such as London, New York, and Moscow.

No doubt in an H-bomb war great cities would be obliterated. But this is one of the minor disasters that would have to be faced. If everybody in London, New York, and Moscow were exterminated the world might, in the course of a few centuries, recover from the blow. But we now know, especially since the Bikini test, that nuclear bombs can gradually spread destruction over a very much wider area than had been supposed.

It is stated on very good authority that a bomb can now be manufactured which will be 2,500 times as powerful as that which destroyed Hiroshima. Such a bomb, if exploded near the ground or under water, sends radio-active particles into the upper air. They sink gradually and reach the sur-face of the earth in the form of a deadly dust or rain. It was this dust which infected the Japanese fishermen and their catch of fish.

No one knows how widely such lethal radio-active par-ticles might be diffused, but the best authorities are unani-mous in saying that a war with H-bombs might quite possibly put an end to the human race. It is feared that if many H-bombs are used there will be universal death – sudden only for a minority, but for the majority a slow torture of disease and disintegration.

Many warnings have been uttered by eminent men of science and by authorities in military strategy. None of them will say that the worst results are certain. What they do say is that these results are possible, and no one can be sure that they will not be realized. We have not yet found that the views of experts on this question depend in any degree upon their politics or prejudices. They depend only, so far as our researches have revealed, upon the extent of the particular expert's knowledge. We have found that the men who know most are the most gloomy.

Here, then, is the problem which we present to you, stark and dreadful and inescapable: Shall we put an end to the human race; or shall mankind renounce war?* People will not face this alternative because it is so difficult to abolish war.

The abolition of war will demand distasteful limitations of national sovereignty.† But what perhaps impedes understanding of the situation more than anything else is that the term 'mankind' feels vague and abstract. People scarcely realize in imagination that the danger is to themselves and their children and their grandchildren, and not only to a dimly apprehended humanity. They can scarcely bring themselves to grasp that they, individually, and those whom they love are in imminent danger of perishing agonizingly. And so they hope that perhaps war may be allowed to continue provided modern weapons are prohibited.

This hope is illusory. Whatever agreements not to use H-bombs had been reached in time of peace, they would no longer be considered binding in time of war, and both sides would set to work to manufacture H-bombs as soon as war broke out, for, if one side manufactured the bombs and the other did not, the side that manufactured them would inevitably be victorious.

Although an agreement to renounce nuclear weapons as

* Professor Joliot-Curie wishes to add the words: 'as a means of settling differences between States.'

† Professor Joliot-Curie wishes to add that these limitations are to be agreed by all and in the interests of all.

part of a general reduction of armaments * would not afford an ultimate solution, it would serve certain important purposes. First: any agreement between East and West is to the good in so far as it tends to diminish tension. Second: the abolition of thermo-nuclear weapons, if each side believed that the other had carried it out sincerely, would lessen the fear of a sudden attack in the style of Pearl Harbor, which at present keeps both sides in a state of nervous apprehension. We should therefore welcome such an agreement, though only as a first step.

Most of us are not neutral in feeling, but, as human beings, we have to remember that, if the issues between East and West are to be decided in any manner that can give any possible satisfaction to anybody, whether Communist or anti-Communist, whether Asian or European or American, whether White or Black, then these issues must not be decided by war. We should wish this to be understood, both in the East and in the West.

There lies before us, if we choose, continual progress in happiness, knowledge, and wisdom. Shall we, instead, choose death, because we cannot forget our quarrels? We appeal, as human beings, to human beings: Remember your humanity, and forget the rest. If you can do so, the way lies open to a new Paradise; if you cannot, there lies before you the risk of universal death.

It was proposed that a conference of scientists should be called, and should vote on a Resolution more or less in the following terms:

RESOLUTION

We invite this Congress, and through it the scientists of the world and the general public, to subscribe to the following resolution:

---

* Professor Muller makes the reservation that this be taken to mean 'a concomitant balanced reduction of all armaments'.

'In view of the fact that in any future world war nuclear weapons will certainly be employed, and that such weapons threaten the continued existence of mankind, we urge the Governments of the world to realize, and to acknowledge publicly, that their purposes cannot be furthered by a world war, and we urge them, consequently, to find peaceful means for the settlement of all matters of dispute between them.'

The spirit of this Resolution governed subsequent Pugwash Conferences.

The signatories of the whole document were:

PROFESSOR MAX BORN (Professor of Theoretical Physics at Berlin, Frankfurt, and Göttingen; Professor of Natural Philosophy, Edinburgh, 1936–53; Nobel Prize in physics).

PROFESSOR P. W. BRIDGMAN (Professor, Harvard University; Nobel Prize in physics).

PROFESSOR ALBERT EINSTEIN.

PROFESSOR L. INFELD (Professor, University of Warsaw; Member of Polish Academy of Sciences; joint author with Einstein of *The Evolution of Physics* and of *The Problem of Motion*).

PROFESSOR J. F. JOLIOT-CURIE (Professor at the Collège de France; Member of the Institut and of the Academy of Medicine; President of the World Federation of Scientific Workers; Nobel Prize in chemistry).

PROFESSOR H. J. MULLER (Formerly a Professor in Moscow, India, etc.; now a Professor at University of Indiana; Nobel Prize in physiology and medicine).

PROFESSOR LINUS PAULING (Director of the Gates & Crellin Laboratories, California Institute of Technology; Nobel Prize in chemistry).

PROFESSOR C. F. POWELL (Professor, Bristol University; Nobel Prize in physics).

PROFESSOR J. ROTBLAT (Professor of Physics, University of London; Medical College of St Bartholomew's Hospital).

BERTRAND RUSSELL.

PROFESSOR HIDEKI YUKAWA (Professor, Kyoto University; Nobel Prize in physics).

This statement I sent about to the various Heads of States with the following letter:

Dear ....

I enclose a statement, signed by some of the most eminent scientific authorities on nuclear warfare, pointing out the danger of utter and irretrievable disaster which would be involved in such warfare, and the consequent necessity of finding some way other than war by which international disputes can be settled. It is my earnest hope that you will give public expression to your opinion as to the problem dealt with in this statement, which is the most serious that has ever confronted the human race.

Yours faithfully
(signed) Bertrand Russell

At the time of publication, there were eleven signatories (two of them with slight reservations). The statement called for an international conference of scientists from East and West and uncommitted nations, alike. The chief difficulty in inaugurating such a conference was financial, since few scientists could afford to pay their own fares. It had been decided that no contributions should be accepted from any already established organized body, but the difficulty was met by the generosity of Cyrus Eaton, who placed his estate at Pugwash, Nova

Scotia, at the disposition of the congress, and helped by generous contributions to the necessary funds. It was found, as had been hoped, that, when the scientists from many countries and of many different political opinions met in an atmosphere of friendly social intercourse, a far greater measure of agreement proved possible than had been achieved at any of the official discussions inaugurated by Governments. After the first conference, a continuing committee was formed to organize future conferences. In addition to small conferences dealing with special points, it was decided to hold large conferences embracing economic and sociological problems, and not to confine invitations to pure scientists, but to include sociologists and economists and others whose opinions might be valuable. Six of these conferences have so far been held,* and it has been found possible to draw up reports in which there was unanimity which included representatives from countries of the Communist bloc as well as those from the West and from uncommitted countries. As one of the most noteworthy, I will quote parts of 'The Vienna Declaration' of 20 September 1958, adopted by the third Pugwash Conference unanimously except for one American participant who abstained. This declaration said (in part):

We meet in Kitzbühel and in Vienna at a time when it has become evident that the development of nuclear weapons

* It is to be noted that by no means all these conferences are held at Pugwash, and that by no means all the conferences held at Pugwash have any connexion with what is known as The Pugwash Movement. A history of The Pugwash Movement, by Professor Rotblat, will shortly be published. I should like to emphasize that his work throughout has been of paramount importance.

makes it possible for man to destroy civilization and, indeed, himself; the means of destruction are being made ever more efficient. The scientists attending our meetings have long been concerned with this development, and they are un- animous in the opinion that a full-scale nuclear war would be a world-wide catastrophe of unprecedented magni- tude.

In our opinion defence against nuclear attack is very difficult. Unfounded faith in defensive measures may even contribute to an outbreak of war.

Although the nations may agree to eliminate nuclear weapons and other weapons of mass destruction from the arsenals of the world, the knowledge of how to produce such weapons can never be destroyed. They remain for all time a potential threat for mankind. In any future major war, each belligerent state will feel not only free but com- pelled to undertake immediate production of nuclear weapons; for no state, when at war, can be sure that such steps are not being taken by the enemy. We believe that, in such a situation, a major industrial power would require less than one year to begin accumulating atomic weapons. From then on, the only restraint against their employment in war would be agreements not to use them, which were concluded in times of peace. The decisive power of nuclear weapons, however, would make the temptation to use them almost irresistible, particularly to leaders who are facing defeat. It appears, therefore, that atomic weapons are likely to be employed in any future major war, with all their terrible consequences.

It is sometimes suggested that localized wars, with limited objectives, might still be fought without catastrophic con- sequences. History shows, however, that the risk of local conflicts growing into major wars is too great to be accept- able in the age of weapons of mass destruction. Mankind must therefore set itself the task of eliminating all wars, including local wars.

The armaments race is the result of distrust between states; it also contributes to this distrust. Any step that mitigates the arms race, and leads to even small reductions in armaments and armed forces, on an equitable basis and subject to necessary control, is therefore desirable. We welcome all steps in this direction and, in particular, the recent agreement in Geneva between representatives of East and West about the feasibility of detecting test-explosions. As scientists, we take particular pleasure in the fact that this unanimous agreement, the first after a long series of unsuccessful international disarmament negotiations, was made possible by mutual understanding and a common objective approach by scientists from different countries. We note with satisfaction that the Governments of the U.S.A., U.S.S.R., and U.K. have approved the statements and the conclusion contained in the report of the technical experts. This is a significant success; we most earnestly hope that this approval will soon be followed by an international agreement leading to the cessation of all nuclear weapon tests and an effective system of control. This would be a first step toward the relaxation of international tension and the end of the arms race. . . .

Our conclusions about the possible consequences of war have been supported by reports and papers submitted to our Conference. These documents indicate that if, in a future war, a substantial proportion of the nuclear weapons already manufactured were delivered against urban targets, most centres of civilization in the belligerent countries would be totally destroyed, and most of their populations killed. This would be true whether the bombs used derived most of their power from fusion reactions (so-called 'clean' bombs) or principally from fission reactions (so-called 'dirty' bombs). In addition to destroying major centres of population and industry, such bombs would also wreck the economy of the country attacked, through the destruction of vital means of distribution and communication.

Major states have already accumulated large stocks of 'dirty' nuclear weapons; it appears that they are continuing to do so. From a strictly military point of view, dirty bombs have advantages in some situations; this makes likely their use in a major war.

The local fall-out resulting from extensive use of 'dirty' bombs would cause the death of a large part of the population in the country attacked. Following their explosion in large numbers (each explosion equivalent to that of millions of tons of ordinary chemical explosive) radio-active fall-out would be distributed, not only over the territory to which they were delivered but, in varying intensity, over the rest of the earth's surface. Many millions of deaths would thus be produced, not only in belligerent but also in non-belligerent countries, by the acute effects of radiation.

There would be, further, substantial long-term radiation damage, to human and other organisms everywhere, from somatic effects such as leukemia, bone cancer, and shortening of the lifespan; and from genetic damage affecting the hereditary traits transmitted to the progeny. ...

It goes without saying that the biological damage from a war, in which many nuclear bombs would be used, would be incomparably larger than that from tests; the main immediate problem before mankind is thus the establishment of conditions that would eliminate war.

We believe that, as scientists, we have an imporant contribution to make towards establishing trust and cooperation among nations. Science is, by long tradition, an international undertaking. Scientists with different national allegiances easily find a common basis of understanding: they use the same concepts and the same methods; they work towards common intellectual goals, despite differences in philosophical, economic, or political views. The rapidly growing importance of science in the affairs of mankind increases the importance of the community of understanding. The ability of scientists all over the world to understand one another, and to work together, is an excellent instrument for bridging the gap between nations and for uniting them around common aims. We believe that working together in every field where international cooperation proves possible makes an important contribution toward establishing an appreciation of the community of nations. It can contribute to the development of the climate of mutual trust, which is necessary for the resolution of political conflicts between nations, and which is an essential background to effective disarmament. We hope scientists everywhere will recognize their responsibility, to mankind and to their own nations, to contribute thought, time, and energy to the furthering of international cooperation. ...

It is our belief that science can best serve mankind, if it is free from interference by any dogma imposed from the outside, and if it exercises its right to question all postulates, including its own. ...

In the present conditions of distrust between nations, and of the race for military supremacy which arises from it, all branches of science – physics, chemistry, biology, psychology – have become increasingly involved in military developments. In the eyes of the people of many countries, science has become associated with the development of weapons. Scientists are either admired for their contribution to national security, or damned for having brought mankind into jeopardy by their invention of weapons of mass destruction. The increasing material support which science now enjoys in many countries is mainly due to its importance, direct or indirect, to the military strength of the nation and to its degree of success in the arms race. This diverts science from its true purpose, which is to increase human knowledge, and to promote man's mastery over the forces of nature for the benefit of all.

We deplore the conditions which lead to this situation,

and appeal to all peoples and their governments to establish conditions of lasting and stable peace.' *

The Pugwash Movement has recently been honoured by the Senate Internal Security Committee (a sub-committee of the Judiciary Committee of the United States Senate). The report of this committee is a truly astonishing document. It regards it as self-evident that any person in the West who wishes to diminish East–West tension must be actuated by pro-Communist bias; that in any more or less friendly contact between any Communist and any non-Communist, the Communist must be capable of outwitting the non-Communist, however great may be the ability of the latter; that any Communist participant in Pugwash conferences must only express the policy of his Government; but that, nevertheless, in spite of Pugwash pronouncements in favour of peace, which Communists have signed, the Russian Government is bent on war. The report allows itself a resort to tricks which is really surprising. In an account of me, it quotes my statement: 'We have to learn to ask ourselves not what steps can be taken to give military victory to whatever group we prefer, for there no longer are such steps' – but this last phrase it omits. It points out that my views on policy were not the same in 1948 as in 1959, and

* This Declaration was signed by one scientist from Australia, Austria, Bulgaria, Denmark, the German Democratic Republic, Hungary, the Netherlands, Norway, Poland, Yugoslavia, respectively; by two from Canada, Czechoslovakia, and Italy; three from India; four from France; five from the Federal Republic of Germany, and Japan; seven from Great Britain; ten from the u.s.s.r.; and twenty from the u.s.a.

I wish to call attention particularly to the paragraph emphasizing the importance of freedom from dogma, which was signed by all ten participants from the u.s.s.r.

benevolently suggests 'that, in 1948, Russell was only seventy-six years old, while in 1959 he was eighty-seven'. It omits to mention that, during the intervening years, another change had taken place, possibly even more important than my further descent towards senility–namely, that, at the earlier date, America alone had the A-bomb, whereas, at the later date, both America and Russia had the H-bomb. It proceeds to point out that there were Communists at the Pugwash Conferences, as though that fact alone discredited them. The aim of diminishing East–West tension, which could not well be pursued in the absence of Communists, was evidently regarded as, in itself, reprehensible. Moscow's approval of Pauling's book *No More War* is quoted as showing Pauling's wickedness, on the ground, apparently, that no right-minded person could oppose nuclear war.

All these, however, are minor criticisms which might amount to no more than evidence that Western scientists, as the report says, are simple-minded folk, 'who blissfully believe that Soviet participation was motivated purely by a scholarly desire to further the cause of international science or by an idealistic urge to advance the movement towards disarmament and international peace.' The eagle eyes of the Senate Internal Security Committee have pierced deeper into the hidden motives of Pugwash scientists. There is a section of the report entitled 'Incitement to Treasonable Action'. This gives an account of the activities of Alan Nunn May, Julius Rosenberg, and Klaus Fuchs, intended to give the reader the impression that these 'traitors' were somehow connected with Pugwash. I have seldom come across a piece of propaganda more dishonest than this.

The whole tone of the report is to the effect that the

wicked Russians praise peace, while all patriotic Americans praise war. Any unprejudiced person, reading the Report and believing it, would inevitably be driven to the support of Russia. Fortunately the West is not quite so black as it is represented to be in this report. But it would be very unwise to overlook the fact that Senate Committees have immense powers of persecution, and use these powers, in the main, to discourage and discredit every approach towards sanity.

6 *Long-term Conditions of Human Survival*

IN this chapter, I shall ask the reader to forget, for the moment, the details of recent history and the political probabilities of the near future. I shall ask him, also, to forget his likes and dislikes, his preferences and aversions, and moral convictions as to what is good or bad. I wish to consider in this chapter, in a purely scientific and impartial manner, what conditions will have to be fulfilled if men are to continue to exist for a long time. So far as physical conditions are concerned, there seems to be no good reason why life, including human life, should not continue for many millions of years. The danger comes, not from man's physical or biological environment, but from himself. He has survived, hitherto, through ignorance. Can he continue to survive now that the useful degree of ignorance is lost?

There is one form of somewhat temporary survival which is not wholly improbable. It may be that a nuclear war in the near future will leave some survivors, but none of the apparatus of civilization. The survivors may, for a long time, be almost entirely occupied in getting food. They may be totally destitute of social institutions and completely unable to transmit knowledge or technique to coming generations. In such conditions, men might repeat the history of the last hundred thousand years, and, having arrived at last at our present degree of wisdom, might once again precipitate their own downfall by a folly equal to our own. This is one possible form of human survival, but it is not one that affords much comfort.

Assuming that men remain capable of scientific technique, what ways are possible by which they might escape from total destruction? We are now asking a narrower question than 'can man survive?' We are now asking 'can *scientific* man survive?' I am not asking merely whether he can survive for the next ten years, or even the next hundred years. He might, by means of expedients and by the help of luck, survive through periods of great danger. But good luck cannot be expected to last for ever, and the dangers which are allowed to persist will sooner or later bring retribution.

For such reasons, I am afraid it must be taken as practically certain that scientific man will not long survive if present international anarchy persists. So long as armed forces are under the command of single nations, or groups of nations, not strong enough to have unquestioned control over the whole world – so long, it is almost certain that sooner or later there will be war, and, so long as scientific technique persists, war will grow more and more deadly. There are already possibilities from which even advocates of H-bombs shrink. The 'Doomsday Machine', which could exterminate us all, could already be constructed. For aught we know, it *has* already been constructed. The cheapest form so far proposed is the Cobalt bomb. This is exactly like the present H-bomb, except that the outer integument consists of cobalt and not of uranium. This would produce by its explosion a radioactive form of cobalt which would decay slowly. If enough Cobalt bombs were exploded, the whole population of the globe would perish within a few years. According to Linus Pauling, in an article in *The Humanist* for March–April 1961: 'For six billion dollars – one-twentieth of the amount spent on armaments each year by the nations of the world – enough Cobalt bombs could be built to ensure the death of every person on earth. . . . No matter what sort of protection were to be devised, it is highly unlikely that any human being would remain alive.'

The Cobalt bomb is only one method of extermination. Present skills could construct many more, and present Governments would be not unlikely to use some of them.

For such reasons, it seems indubitable that scientific man cannot long survive unless all the major weapons of war, and all the means of mass determination, are in the hands of a single Authority, which, in consequence of its monopoly, would have irresistible power and, if challenged to war, could wipe out any rebellion within a few days without much damage except to the rebels. This, it seems plain, is an absolutely indispensable condition of the continued existence of a world possessed of scientific skill.

There are various ways in which such a world might come about. Until both sides had the H-bomb, it might have come about as the result of a nuclear war in which one side was victorious and was able to impose its will without the means of successful resistance. This possibility no longer exists. What exact degree of damage would be done by a nuclear war with present weapons is uncertain, and we must all hope that it will remain so. It is just possible that, after a nuclear war between NATO and the Powers of the Warsaw Pact, some neutral nations might retain a degree of social cohesion which would enable them to keep civilization alive. If, for example, China were to remain prudently neutral in such a war and if the wind blew from the East throughout the few days of its continuation, China might be in a position to claim world-dominion. If China were a belligerent, or if the wind were westerly, the Empire of the world might fall to an alliance of South Africa and Australia. In any of these events, the surviving nation, or nations, might compel the few remnants of the populations in what had been the Great Powers to submit and be ruled despotically in a world where resistance to the power of surviving nations would be impossible.*

This is one way in which, conceivably, the world might be governmentally unified. It is not a very pleasant way, and it is certainly not the way that any of the present nuclear Powers would welcome. I do not think, however, that such a result of a nuclear war is at all probable. It seems very much more likely that civilized existence would become impossible in the countries which had been neutrals as well as in the belligerent countries.

A much more desirable way of securing world peace would be by a voluntary agreement among nations to pool their armed forces and submit to an agreed International Authority. This may seem, at present, a distant and Utopian prospect, but there are practical politicians who think otherwise. Mr Macmillan, when he was Minister of Defence and speaking on behalf of the Government, said: 'On the whole question of disarmament our purpose is simple and our record is clear. Genuine disarmament must be based on two simple but vital principles. It must be comprehensive, by which I mean that it must include all weapons, new and old, conventional and unconventional. The control must provide effective international, or if we like supranational, authority in-

* In my book called *Power*, published in 1938, I said: 'A world State is now a technical possibility, and might be established by a victor in some really serious world war, or, more probably, by the most powerful of the neutrals' (p. 173).

vested with real power. Hon. Members may say that this is elevating the United Nations, or whatever may be the authority, into something like world government; be it so, it is none the worse for that. In the long run this is the only way out for mankind.' *

I could mention a number of other men, neither Utopian nor destitute of political experience, who have expressed similar opinions. But for the present, I am not concerned with the practical possibility of creating a World Government, but with the continued existence of civilized society.

A World Government of a sort might be created without securing world peace. This might happen, for example, if the various nations which contributed to the armed force of the World Authority did so by supplying national contingents which might retain their national unity and, at a crisis, might be loyal to their national Government rather than to the World Authority. It may be worth while to give an outline of a possible World Constitution especially designed to obviate such dangers. Such an outline is, of course, only a suggestion, and emphatically not a prophecy. My purpose is merely to show that a World Constitution which would prevent war is possible.

A World Authority, if it is to fulfil its function, must have a legislature and an executive and irresistible military power. Irresistible military power is the most essential condition and also the most difficult to fulfil. I will, therefore, deal with it first.

All nations would have to agree to reduce national armed forces to the level necessary for internal police action. No nation should be allowed to retain nuclear

* House of Commons, March 1955.

weapons or any other means of wholesale destruction.
The World Authority should have power to recruit in
every country and to manufacture such weapons as might
be deemed essential. In a world where separate nations
were disarmed, the military forces of the World Authority
would not need to be very large and would not constitute
an onerous burden upon the various constituent nations.
In order to prevent the development of national loyalties
in any part of the international forces, it would be necessary that each fairly large unit should be of mixed
nationality. There should not be European contingents or
Asian contingents or African contingents or American
contingents, but there should be everywhere, as far as
possible, a balanced mixture. The higher commands
should, as far as possible, be given to men from small
countries which could not entertain any hope of world
dominion. There would, of course, have to be a right of
inspection by the World Government to make sure that
the disarmament provisions in every country were obeyed.

The constitution of the legislature would, of course, be
federal. Separate nations should preserve their autonomy
in everything that did not concern war or peace. There is,
in any federal constitution, a difficulty where the units
are of very different sizes. Should each unit have the
same voice, or should voting power be proportional to
population? In America, as everyone knows, an in-
genious compromise was adopted: one principle governed the Senate and the other the House of Representatives. I think, however, that a different principle would
work better in constructing the world legislature. I think
there should be subordinate federations of approximately
equal population. These should be constructed, as far as
possible, so as to be fairly homogeneous and to have

many common interests. Wherever a number of States were combined in one of these subordinate federations, the World Authority should take cognizance only of the external relations of federations and not of the relations between different States in one federation unless a risk of war was involved or some unconstitutional action.

How these federations should be constituted would no doubt vary with the time that the constitution was enacted. If it were enacted at the present time, one might suggest some such arrangement as the following: (1) China; (2) India and Ceylon; (3) Japan and Indonesia; (4) the Mohammedan world from Pakistan to Morocco; (5) Equatorial Africa; (6) the U.S.S.R. and Satellites; (7) Western Europe, Britain, Ireland, and Australia and New Zealand; (8) the U.S.A. and Canada; (9) Latin America. Some countries which do not come in this division present difficulties. For example, Jugoslavia, Israel, South Africa, and Korea. It is impossible to guess, in advance, what might, at any given moment, be the best arrangement for such countries. Each federation should be represented in the world legislature in proportion to its population. There would have to be both a world constitution setting out the relations of the subordinate federations to the world federation, and also a constitution of each subordinate federation guaranteed by the world federation. The World Government would support subordinate federations and their constituent States in any constitutional action. It should only interfere with the internal affairs of the subordinate federations in the event of a federation engaging in some unconstitutional action; and the same principle should apply to the relations between a subordinate federation and its constituent national States.

What should be the powers of the world legislature? In the first place, no treaty should be valid unless confirmed by the legislature, which should also have power to revise existing treaties if new circumstances made this advisable. The legislature should also have the right to object to violently nationalist systems of education such as might be considered to constitute a danger to peace.

There would need to be, also, an executive which, I think, should be responsible to the legislature. Its main function, apart from maintaining the armed forces, should be to declare any violation of the world constitution by any national State or combination of States and, if necessary, to inflict punishment for such violation.

There is one other matter of very considerable importance, and that is international law. At present, international law has very little force. It would be essential that a legal institution like The Hague Court should have the same authority as belongs to national courts. I think, further, that there should be an international criminal law for dealing with men who have committed crimes that were popular in their own country. In the Nuremberg Trials, it was impossible to feel the justice of sentences inflicted as a result of victory in war, although it was also clear that there ought to have been a legal method of punishing at least some of those who were condemned.

I think that, if such an International Authority is to be successful in diminishing motives towards warlike feelings, it will have to work to promote a continual approach towards economic equality in the standard of life of different parts of the world. So long as there are rich countries and poor countries, there will be envy on the one side and possible economic oppression on the other.

A continual attempt to move towards economic equality must, therefore, be part of the pursuit of secure and lasting peace.

Many powerful objections to World Government, of no matter what kind, are, as yet, very widely felt. I shall deal with these in the next chapter.

7 *Why World Government is Disliked*

THE chief argument in favour of World Government is that, if suitably constituted, it can prevent war. It would, however, be quite easy to construct a supranational organization which might be *called* a World Government, but would not effectively prevent war. Such a Government would encounter much less opposition than one in which all serious armed force was under the command of the World Government. Since this is an essential condition for the long-term prevention of war, I shall not dignify anything less by the name of World Government. It is objections to the kind of system suggested in the preceding chapter that I am now concerned to consider.

Much the strongest objections arise from the sentiment of nationalism. When we say, 'Britons never, never shall be slaves', our hearts swell with pride and we feel, though we do not explicitly say, that we should be slaves if we were not free at any moment to commit any crime against any other country. The feeling in favour of national freedom is one which has been rapidly increasing throughout the last hundred and fifty years, and, if World Government is to be inaugurated, it will have to take account of this sentiment and do whatever is possible to satisfy it.

The men who argue in favour of unrestricted national freedom do not realize that the same reasons would justify unrestricted individual freedom. I will not yield to Patrick Henry, or anyone else, in love of freedom, but, if there is to be as much freedom in the world as possible, it is necessary that there should be restrictions preventing violent assaults upon the freedom of others. In the internal affairs of States this is recognized: murder is everywhere made illegal. If the law against murder were repealed, the liberty of all except murderers would be diminished, and even the liberty of murderers would, in most cases, be short-lived, since they would soon be murdered. But, although everyone, except a few anarchists, admits this as regards the relations of an individual to his national State, there is immense reluctance to admit it as regards the relations of national States to the world at large.

It is true that attempts have been made, ever since the time of Grotius, to create a body of international law. These attempts have been wholly admirable; and, in so far as international law has commanded general respect, it has been useful. But it has remained optional with each national State to respect or not respect codes of international law. Law is a farce unless there is power to enforce it, and power to enforce international law against great States is impossible while each possesses vast armaments. Great States have, at present, the privilege of killing members of other States whenever they feel so disposed, though this liberty is disguised as the heroic privilege of dying in defence of what is right and just. Patriots always talk of dying for their country, and never of killing for their country.

War has so long been a part of human life that it is difficult for our feelings and our imaginations to grasp that the present anarchic national freedoms are likely to result in freedom only for corpses. If institutions could be created which would prevent war, there would be much more freedom in the world than there is at present, just as there is more freedom owing to the prevention of individual murder.

Nevertheless, while the sentiment of nationalism remains as strong as it is at present, effective restrictions
of the national sovereignty will continue to be distasteful to a great many people. Suppose, for example,
that there was only one navy in the world, and that its
supreme admiral should be chosen in rotation from the
various participating Powers. Most patriotic Britons
would exclaim: 'What, should the British Navy, which
Nelson led to glory, come in due course to be commanded by a Russian! Perish the thought!' And after
this exclamation, the man who had made it would become impervious to further argument. He would go on
to point out that an international force might be employed against his own country. Most countries have,
at one time or another, committed acts which a World
Government would have to pronounce criminal, and
some of the worst offenders in this respect have been
admired by people who considered themselves liberal.
The most noteworthy example in history is the admiration of Napoleon by men like Byron and Heine. Before
a World Government becomes possible, it will be necessary that men be made to realize the impossibility of
international anarchy while modern weapons of mass
destruction exist. This is a difficult task and is not rendered easier by the opposition of powerful Governments.

Another objection to World Government which is at
present very powerful, especially in Communist countries, is that it might stereotype the *status quo*. So long
as the opposition between Communists and anti-Communists remains as fierce as it is at present, it will be
difficult to win assent to any international institutions
which might seem likely to impede the transition of in-

dividual nations from one camp to the other. It would, of course, be possible to decree that each nation should be free to arrange its own economy in whatever way it pleased, but it might prove exceedingly difficult to secure that this liberty should be genuinely respected. If World Government is to be successfully established, there will have to be much more tolerance than there is at present between different kinds of national government. It will be necessary to forgo some part of the pleasures of national self-assertion. Each nation may continue to *think*, as each nation does at present, that it is superior to all other nations in every essential respect, but, when nations meet for purposes of negotiation, the negotiators will have to restrain the public expression of their feelings of superiority within the limits of courtesy. Such restraint would not be easy while national sentiments remain as strong as they are at present.

There is another argument which is often used against World Government. It is said, and widely believed, that it would bring a new danger of military tyranny. What would prevent the international armed force from making a military insurrection, and installing its general-issimo as Emperor of the World? Those who bring up this argument fail to realize that exactly the same problem exists at present in every national State. It is a very real problem, and in many countries, though not in the most civilized, military tyrannies have been established by unconstitutional methods. But in the leading countries of the world, control over the military by the civil authorities has been pretty successfully maintained. When Lincoln was appointing a Commander-in-Chief over the Northern forces in the American Civil War, he was warned that the candidate whom he favoured would

seek dictatorship. Lincoln wrote to him, mentioning
these fears, and added: 'The way to become a dictator
is to win victories. I shall look to you for the victories,
and I will risk the dictatorship.' Events proved that this
was a wise decision. In the conflict in England over the
Reform Bill, Wellington was passionately opposed to
reform, but, in spite of his immense reputation, it never
occurred to him to lead the Army against Parliament.
In Russia, when Stalin turned against a number of
Generals, he had no difficulty in having them executed.
The superiority of the civil government over the armed
forces in the U.S.S.R. has been complete ever since the
end of the civil war which gave power to the Soviet
Government. There is no reason to suppose that it
would be more difficult to keep the military in order
under a World Government than it is under national
governments. The danger is one of which the civil government would have to be aware, but there is no reason
to think that the methods which would be developed
for combating the danger would be less successful than
they have proved in the great States of the present day.

There would have to be, everywhere, but especially
in the armed forces, a vigorous inculcation of loyalty to
the World Government. If, as was suggested in the previous chapter, every large unit in the armed forces was
of completely mixed nationality, it would be difficult, if
not impossible, for a faction to generate a spirit of
nationalistic revolt.

There is one rather grave psychological obstacle to
the establishment of a World Government. It is that
there would be no outside enemy to fear. Social cohesion, in so far as it is instinctive, is mainly promoted
by a common danger or a common enmity. This is most

obvious where a grown-up person is in charge of a number of unruly children. So long as everything remains quiet, it is difficult to get the children to obey, but if anything frightening happens, such as a bad thunderstorm or a fierce dog, the children instantly seek the protection of the grown-up and become completely obedient. The same sort of thing applies to adults, though not quite so obviously. Patriotism is far more intense in time of war than at other times, and there is a readiness to obey even onerous governmental decrees which is absent when there is secure peace. A World Government, since it would have no external human enemies, would not be able to invoke quite this motive for loyalty. I think it would be necessary, as an essential part of education, to remind people of the dangers that would still remain, such as poverty and malnutrition and epidemics, and, also, to make them aware that, if loyalty to the World Government failed, scientific war might once more become probable. Although hatred of foreign nations promotes social cohesion more easily, perhaps, than anything else, it would be unduly pessimistic to suppose that nothing more positive and more beneficial could take its place. This whole matter is one which depends more upon education than upon anything else. I shall return to it in a subsequent chapter.

So far, I have been considering the psychological obstacles to World Government, but, as against these, all technical developments since the Industrial Revolution have afforded reasons for increase in the size of States and, since our planet is finite in size, these technical reasons lead very powerfully towards a unified Government of the whole world. The size of States in the past has been governed in the main by an equilibrium be-

tween two opposing forces: on the one hand, love of
power on the part of the government; and, on the other,
love of independence on the part of the governed. The
point at which these two forces find themselves in equilibrium at any given stage of development depends mainly
upon technique. Increase in the speed of mobility, and
increase in the cost of weapons, both tend towards
larger governmental units. Where weapons are cheap and
mobility is slow a large governmental unit is apt to be
unstable when faced with local revolt. For this reason,
there has, on the whole, been a tendency for States to
grow larger when civilization is advancing, and smaller
when civilization is decaying. Some of the earliest events
in recorded history are concerned with early amalgama-
tions of previously hostile Governments. The oldest civilization known through records, and not only through
archaeology, is that of Egypt. Originally, Upper and
Lower Egypt were completely independent of each other,
but they were united into one kingdom somewhere about
the year 3,500 B.C. This unification was facilitated by the
Nile, which made communication between different parts
of Egypt easy and, for those times, fairly swift. The same
sort of thing happened in Mesopotamia. Originally, there
were two very distinct groups, one called Sumer and the
other called Akkad. These two were completely distinct
in race, religion, and language. At last they were unified
by a great conqueror, Sargon, or possibly by his immediate successors. According to the *Cambridge Ancient
History* (Vol. I, p. 38) this happened about the year 2,872
B.C. The increased power which resulted from unification
led gradually to the creation of the Babylonian Empire.
For those days, this Empire was very large, though it
would not seem so by modern standards. The first really

large Empire in history was that of Persia which, like those of Egypt and Mesopotamia, resulted from the union of two previously hostile groups, the Medes and the Persians. The ability of a single central government to control the whole area depended upon roads. In those days, and, in fact, until the nineteenth century, neither men nor goods nor news could travel faster than a horse. The Persians were the first to construct great roads, more especially the road from Sardis to Suza which was about 1,500 miles long. A messenger on horseback could cover this distance in a month, but for an army with baggage, the journey took about three months. In consequence of this, when the Ionian Greeks rebelled against Persia, they had plenty of time to make their preparations, and, although they were defeated in the end, it was with great difficulty. Persian dependence upon roads was inherited by the Macedonians, but it was the Romans who brought it to perfection. Rome, until it was overthrown, brought to its subjects many of the benefits for which, now, we must look to World Government. A man could travel from Britain to the Euphrates without ever coming across a frontier or a customs barrier. The civilization of this enormous area was completely unified, and for a long time it did not seem as if Rome had anything to fear from outside nations. When Rome fell, an opposite process to that which had marked the growth of civilization hitherto, set in. A large number of small and mutually hostile States replaced the previous unified Government. The level of civilization fell catastrophically, and the roads, upon which Roman power had depended, were allowed to fall into decay.

Gradually, however, a new movement towards a more civilized order began. In England, where there had been a number of separate kings, and where, for example, Mercia and Wessex had hated each other as bitterly as Russia and America do now, unification was accomplished by Alfred the Great. Some 700 years later, England and Scotland, which had fought each other for centuries, were united by a dynastic accident. Perhaps, if Queen Elizabeth I had had children, we might still be fighting Bannockburn and Flodden Field.

The invention of gunpowder not only increased the size of States, but also enormously increased the power of the central Government within each State. The anarchy of feudal nobles in impregnable castles ended with the coming of artillery. Henry VII in England, Richelieu in France, and Ferdinand and Isabella in Spain first established secure internal peace throughout their dominions. This is a noteworthy example of the political effects of a new military technique.

But, although gunpowder made it possible for a Government to control effectively areas as large as France or Spain, it did not create the technical conditions which would have been necessary for a World Government. These have arisen only in our own day. The first necessary step was the rapid transmission of news. Before the invention of the telegraph, an Ambassador was, of necessity, largely independent of the Government that had appointed him, because he had to act on the circumstances of the moment in the country to which he was accredited, and these were not yet known in the country to which he belonged. Railways, also, played a very important part. I think one may reckon that, if Napoleon had had railways, he would have been able to defeat Russia in 1812. But the changes that have taken place during our own century are much more important than either the railway or the telegraph. Of these recent changes, the first was the conquest of the air, which has made it possible to move an army in a few days from any one place to any other. The invention of nuclear weapons has even more importance than the conquest of the air, and, when they are carried by missiles, the time taken in their journey is so short as to seem almost negligible.

These technical advances, while they have made present international anarchy infinitely more dangerous than it used to be, have also made it technically possible to establish a World Government which would be able to exert its power everywhere and could make armed resistance virtually impossible. This new situation is due, in the main, to three scientific novelties: the first and most important of these is the vast destructiveness of modern nuclear weapons; the second is the extreme rapidity with which they can reach their targets; and the third is their immense cost. All these increase the possible size of a stable State. So far, this possible size is confined to the earth's surface, but very soon it may extend to the moon and the planets.

These are possibilities, but only if the human race does not destroy itself by clinging to political forms which modern weapons have rendered obsolete.

8 *First Steps Towards Secure Peace*

THE first steps towards the attainment of secure peace, like the first tottering steps of an infant, will almost necessarily be small and doubtful. In this chapter, I want to consider, not all that is desirable, but all that might conceivably be achieved by negotiators in a not too distant future.

The first thing that is needed is a different atmosphere in debates between East and West. At present these debates are conducted in the spirit of an athletic contest. What each side thinks important is, not the reaching of agreement, but its own victory either in a propaganda performance for the rest of the world or in securing from the other side concessions which might tilt the balance of power in what would be considered a favourable direction. Neither side remembers that the future of man is at stake and that almost any agreement would be better than none. Take, for example, the long-drawn-out negotiations for the abolition of tests. East and West have always agreed that the spread of nuclear weapons to new Powers would increase the likelihood of nuclear war. Both sides have agreed that the spread of nuclear weapons to new Powers is imminent. Both sides have agreed that a ban on nuclear tests would help to prevent this spread. From these premises, both sides have felt, not that tests must stop, but that whichever side is in question must *seem* to wish to stop them. The negotiations began hopefully with a joint declaration of the scientists of East and West that a test anywhere could be detected by the other side. Thereupon, the American Government announced that it needed to make underground tests and that these could easily pass undetected. After some years of negotiation this obstacle was overcome. The Soviet Government thereupon announced that the necessary inspection should not be directed by one man representing the United Nations, but by three men – one East, one West, and one neutral – and that they should only act when there was unanimity. As was to be feared these manoeuvres on the part of America and Russia made the years of negotiation fruitless and led to the resumption of tests by Russia. One cannot but conclude that neither side has been sincere in pretending to wish that tests should cease by agreement.

If any progress is to be made with any of the problems that cause East–West tension, negotiators must meet, not in the hope of outwitting each other, or of prolonging the dangerous *status quo*, but with an absolute determination that agreement should be reached. It must be accepted that an agreement is not likely to be wholly palatable to either party. The aim should be to reach agreements which do not alter the balance of power, but do diminish the risk of war.

I can see only one motive which can lead to this change in the attitude of negotiators. This motive will have to be consciousness on both sides of the futile horror of nuclear war. At present, each side thinks it necessary for success in the war of nerves to pretend that it might win. And not only for success in the war of nerves, but also to lure its own citizens to their death by promises which Governments must know to be deceitful. One side announces, 'We might win a hot war'; the other side retorts, 'We shall obliterate you.' Such statements tend to promote warlike fury in whichever side is threatened. If any steps towards peace are to be achieved, both sides will have to recognize that they face a common peril and that the true enemy is not the other side, but the weapons of mass destruction which both sides possess.

If this is recognized on both sides, the problem becomes a quite different one. It is no longer the problem of outwitting the other side, or of persuading one's own side that it is capable of victory. The first problem will have to be to find *acceptable* steps, however small, which can prove that fruitful negotiations have become possible.

There is a considerable amount of rhetoric, both on the warlike and on the peaceful side, which, whatever its intention, is not likely to lead to the desired result. We have formerly considered the rhetorical war propaganda embodied in the slogan, 'Liberty or Death', but there is an opposite slogan invented by West German friends of peace: 'Better Red than dead.' One may guess that in some sections of Russian public opinion, there is an opposite slogan: 'Better capitalists than corpses.' I do not think it is necessary to inquire into the theoretical validity of either slogan since I think it out of the question that the one should be adopted by Western Governments or the other by the Governments of the East. Neither slogan presents justly the problem which East and West, alike, have to face. Given that military victory by either side is impossible, it follows logically that a negotiated *détente* cannot be based on the complete subjection of either side to the other, but must preserve the existing balance while transforming it from a balance of terror to a balance of hope. That is to say, co-existence must be accepted genuinely and not superficially as a necessary condition of human survival.

Perhaps the first step should be a solemn declaration by the U.S. and the U.S.S.R., and as many other Powers as possible, that a nuclear war would be an utter disaster to both East and West and, also, to neutrals, and that it would not achieve anything that East or West or neutrals could possibly desire. I should hope that such a declaration could be made sincerely. Both sides know that what it would say is true, but both sides are caught in a net of prestige, propaganda, and power politics, from which, hitherto, they have not known how to extricate themselves. I should like to see the neutrals taking the lead in achieving such a declaration, and I do not see how either side could incur the odium of refusing to sign.

The next step should be a temporary moratorium, say for a period of two years, during which each side would pledge itself to abstain from provocative actions. Among provocative actions should be included such measures as interference with the freedom of West Berlin, or intervention by the U.S. in Cuba. It should be agreed that United Nations observers, as impartial as could be found, should decide whether an act is provocative.

During the two years' moratorium, various preliminary steps should be taken with a view to making subsequent negotiations easier. There should be on both sides a discouragement of vehement hostile propaganda and an attempt by means of greatly increased cultural contact to diminish the popular view in East and West of West and East as melodramatic monsters of wickedness. Steps should be taken to lessen the danger of unprovoked or unintended war. At the present time, each side fears an unprovoked attack by the other, and each side has a vast system of detection by which it hopes to discover such an unprovoked attack a few minutes before it occurs.

Each side's methods of detection are fallible and, therefore, each side may believe itself about to be attacked
when nothing of the sort is occurring. If it believes this,
it will order what it supposes to be a counter-attack, but
what, to the other side, will appear merely unprovoked
aggression. This is a mutual nightmare, caused by tension, but immensely increasing it. It is hardly possible
that tension should be very seriously diminished while
both sides live under the threat of 'instant retaliation',
which may well be, not retaliation, but response to a mistake. It is by no means easy to see what can be done
about this situation when it has once been allowed to
grow up. Nuclear disarmament, of course, would solve
this problem. Not long ago the danger might have been
much alleviated by abolition of launching sites, or, if that
were thought too extreme a measure, by making the
launching sites temporarily unavailable. But, since the introduction of submarines provided with nuclear weapons,
launching sites have lost a good deal of their dominant
importance. The diminution of the danger of unintended
or accidental war has become a technical question of
much complexity and, short of nuclear disarmament, it
would seem that only palliatives are possible. If a *détente*
is genuinely desired on both sides, a technical commis-
sion composed of East and West in equal numbers could
be appointed to diminish this danger, but what exactly it
could recommend, it is difficult to decide, and it must
always be remembered that palliatives are unreliable, and
that nuclear disarmament affords the only genuine protection against this danger.

There should also be an attempt on both sides, on the
one hand, to increase mutual knowledge of each other's
case, and, on the other hand, to disseminate information

as to the disastrousness of a nuclear war should it take place.

The main work to be performed during the moratorium would be an agreement to appoint a Conciliation Committee consisting of equal numbers of members from East and West and neutrals. I think such a Committee, if it were to perform its work efficiently, would have to be small. It might, for example, consist of four members from the West, four from the East, and four neutrals. It should – at least, at first – have advisory powers only. Whenever it did not succeed in reaching unanimity, the opinions of both majority and minority, with the reasons for them, should be made public. Its decisions should be governed by certain principles. Of these, the first and most important should be that the proposals as a whole offered no net gain to either side, since, otherwise, there would be no chance of their being agreed to. For example, Russia should cease to jam Western radios provided that they abstained from virulent hostile propaganda. The second principle to be adopted should be to seek ways of diminishing dangerous friction in areas where this is occurring – as, for example, between Israel and the Arab world, or between North and South Korea. A third principle – which, however, should be subordinate to the other two – would be to allow self-determination wherever possible. There are limits to what can be done in this direction since the Russians would not agree to its application in their satellites, and it is doubtful whether the U.S. would agree unreservedly as regards Latin America. As regards Formosa, I have never seen any account of the wishes of the inhabitants or any suggestion by either East or West that respect should be paid to their wishes. Until the world is much less tense than it is at present, the principle of self-determination, desirable as it is, will have to give way, here and there, to considerations of power politics. This is regrettable, but is, I fear, unavoidable if agreement is to be reached between the Great Powers.

There is another matter of very great importance which should be dealt with during the moratorium, and that is the reform and strengthening of the United Nations. UNO ought to be open to every State that wishes to join it, not only China, which is the most urgent, but also East and West Germany. The problem of Germany, however, is very special, and I shall have more to say about it in a later chapter.

UNO is defective, not only because it excludes certain countries, but also because of the Veto. UNO cannot lead on towards a World Government while the Veto is retained, but, on the other hand, it is difficult to abolish the Veto while national armaments retain their present strength. On this point, as in the matter of Germany, the question of disarmament has to be decided before any satisfactory solution is possible.

It is because of the imperfections of UNO that an *ad hoc* Conciliation Committee would, at first, be a better body than UNO for initiating schemes of conciliation. One may hope that, if such a body, while still having only an advisory capacity, did its work wisely, it might, in time, acquire such moral authority as would make its proposals difficult to resist and would give it, in embryo, an influence that might facilitate the ultimate establishment of a World Government. The great advantage of such a body would be that the neutrals would hold the balance between East and West, and, if they thought proposals by one side more reasonable than those by the other, they could give the majority to the side they thought best on the particular issue in question. One would hope that the neutrals would be sometimes on one side and sometimes on the other. Moreover, if one side, but not the other, was in danger of encountering neutral opposition – as would be bound to happen to either side occasionally – this would tend to promote moderation on both sides. The desirability of appealing to neutrals would tend to soften the acerbity of both East and West in discussions, and to generate, gradually, a world-wide point of view, rather than one confined to this side or that. Moreover, where there is a deadlock between East and West, there is better hope of a wise compromise solution being suggested by the neutrals than by either of the contesting parties of East and West. These are, perhaps, the most important things that neutrals can do towards the promotion of sanity. It is largely because I believe that it is neutrals who will have to play the most important role in the preservation of peace that I should wish to see Britain leaving NATO and trying to inspire wise action by a neutral bloc. National pride causes most Britons to think that such action would seriously weaken the West, but this is not the view of authoritative American orthodox experts. Also, paradoxically, it would make it more probable, not less, that some Britons might survive. But the most important argument for British neutrality is the help towards world peace that Britain could do as a neutral, but cannot do as a member of either bloc.

I have not dealt in this chapter either with disarmament or with territorial questions, but only with such preliminary steps as might lessen the hostility between East and West. Both disarmament and territorial questions will be considered in the ensuing chapters.

9 *Disarmament*

GENERAL disarmament, though immensely important and desirable, would not, if achieved, be enough in itself to secure a stable peace. So long as scientific technique continues to be understood, any major war that might break out would lead to the manufacture of nuclear weapons by both sides and of whatever even more deadly weapons had been foreseen during the previous years of peace. But, although disarmament, for this reason, is not alone sufficient, it is a very essential step without which no other can lead to much of value.

Those who favour disarmament often base their case upon the contention that weapons of mass destruction are immoral. Undoubtedly this is true, but so are bows and arrows immoral. There is, it is true, a profound and important difference in degree: if it is wicked to kill one man, it is two hundred million times as wicked to kill two hundred million people. But it is not immorality which is the really novel feature of modern weapons. The really novel feature is the absolute certainty that, in a war, *both* sides will be defeated. It is this that makes all thought of modern war silly as well as wicked. The people, whether in East or West, who tolerate policies leading towards war, are victims of delusion. Some, who advocate Brinkmanship, persuade themselves that in a war of nerves the other side is sure to yield first. This is what Hitler thought after Munich, and his miscalculation led to his downfall. In the same situation at the present day it would have led also to the downfall of his enemies.

There is another group of even more dangerous war-

mongers. These are the people so filled with national or
ideological pride that, in the face of all evidence, they
still believe that their side would 'win'. I think that this
unfounded belief is widely prevalent in both Russia and
America, and is encouraged by the Governments of both
countries as an asset in negotiation.

There is a third group, the group of sacrificial fanatics.
This group holds that it is noble to fight and die in a good
cause even if the result of your sacrifice is going to be a
much worse world than that which would exist if you
were less prepared for martyrdom.

Unfortunately, ever since Hiroshima, these three groups
have acted together and have succeeded, hitherto, in preventing anything that might diminish the risk of nuclear
war. There have been moments, it is true, when one side
or the other showed some glimmerings of common sense,
but never have both sides felt these glimmerings at the
same moment.

The history of disarmament conferences from Hiroshima to the present day is one of the most discouraging
stories in human history. After the dropping of the
atomic bombs on Hiroshima and Nagasaki, it was felt,
even in America (when they had the monopoly), that
atomic energy should be internationalized. The American Government employed Lillienthal to draw up a proposal in this sense for the consideration of the American
Government. It was an admirable proposal, but it was
felt that it could not be offered to other Powers exactly
as it stood. What emerged as an international offer was
the Baruch proposal in which there were certain addi-
tions which, it was hoped, would make the proposal unacceptable to Russia. This hope proved justified.

It must be said that, in the years immediately follow-

ing the end of the Second World War, Stalin did everything in his power to make conciliation impossible.
America, in the year or so after the end of the war, carried out an enormous reduction of conventional arms
without eliciting any response from Stalin. Stalin, on the
contrary, although at Yalta he had undertaken that countries other than Russia in the Eastern sphere should
have democratic Governments, established a rigid military and police dictatorship in all the satellite countries.
When this was followed by the Berlin Blockade and the
Russian acquisition of nuclear weapons, the West settled
down to the Cold War with a hardening of anti-Russian
feeling and policy. When, after the death of Stalin, the
U.S.S.R. made tentative approaches to a lessening of tension, the West received these approaches sceptically. In
spite of disarmament conferences and conferences for
the abolition of tests, nothing whatever has been done –
except, for a time, a moratorium on tests so long as the
conference on tests should continue. Although in early
years after 1945 the chief blame must fall on Russia, this
could not be said until lately of the years after Stalin's
death. On the contrary, when Khrushchev proposed universal and complete disarmament the West cynically dis-
missed his suggestion as a trick. What Western authorities
thought, although this was not exactly what they said in
public, was: 'Khrushchev seems to pretend that the purpose of a disarmament conference is to secure disarmament. He must know perfectly well that this is not the purpose on either side and that the true purpose is merely to
play a propaganda game in which each side can pretend
to want disarmament without incurring any danger of
getting it. His proposal of universal disarmament, as it
stands, is obviously defective as regards inspection. We

make this a reason for rejecting the proposal without first
inquiring whether Khrushchev would agree to amend-
ments obviating this objection.' And so, once more,
nothing is done.

It is recognized on both sides that there would be immense advantages in making what is called the 'first
strike'. If either side makes an unexpected nuclear attack,
it can do so much damage that a really effective second
strike would become very difficult. This is one of the
problems with which Kahn's *Thermonuclear War* is
mainly concerned. Many influential Americans, as well
as many influential people in Western Europe, believe
that such an unprovoked attack by the U.S.S.R. may occur
at any moment. It is to be supposed that the corresponding opinion exists in Russia, and that alertness against
an expected first strike is just as great there as it is in the
West. This mutual alertness not only militates against
any possible *détente*, but also immensely increases the
likelihood of an unintended nuclear war. Seymour Melman, the editor of a very valuable book (*Inspection for
Disarmament*, Columbia University Press, 1958), recog-
nizes this danger and states it with great clarity and emphasis. He says (p. x):

Undoubtedly the designers of nuclear weapons have attempted to build into them certain mechanical safeguards
against accidental firing – such as the requirement for a
deliberate adjustment before such weapons become opera-
tive. There are no final safeguards, however, against the
probability of human failure. As nuclear weapons are produced by the tens of thousands, and must be used by even
more than that many men, the possibilities of world disaster through human failure cannot be ignored. One aber-
rant, psychotic person, or person gone momentarily out of

control, could explode nuclear weapons at a random place, or over any populated area. A space satellite could be mistaken for a ballistic missile.

Since military tactics and technologies have become geared to the idea of rapid retaliation, such accidents would require only one misjudgement in response to set the swift moves and countermoves of catastrophic nuclear war in motion. As nuclear weapons are increasingly available and dispersed in more hands, the probabilities of such an accident must necessarily increase. In the judgement of this writer, such possibilities weaken the assumption of rationally calculated moves among military powers, which underlie the strategies of peace through mutual armed deterrence.

Lastly, one of the major assumptions of the mutual deterrence strategy will be drastically altered when many countries possess nuclear weapons. If a warhead should be set off in some city, it might be impossible to identify the aggressor, because of the number of countries possessing bombs, and the variety of possible ways for delivering nuclear explosives. Unless the aggressor were known, it would be clearly impossible even to threaten retaliation. Thereby, the strategy of a 'balance of terror' fails as a way for deterring nuclear attacks.

This opinion is shared by all who have no political motive for disputing it, and even by some who have – for example, Lord Hailsham, our Minister of Science, says that sooner or later there will be war (*Daily Sketch*, 11 August 1960). C. P. Snow is even more emphatic. He says, 'Within at the most ten years some of those bombs are going off. *That* is a certainty', in an article, 'The Moral Un-neutrality of Science' (*Monthly Review*, February 1961, p. 156). I could give many quotations expressing the same opinion, none of them from extremists.

What does this mean in human terms? The likelihood

of an unprovoked first strike by either Russia or America, probably under the impression that it is a retaliatory strike, is not very great on any one given day, but with each day that passes the same likelihood, whatever it may be, is added and, in the end, becomes almost a certainty unless policies are changed. If C. P. Snow is right – and there is no reason whatever to think him wrong – at some day during the next ten years, H-bombs will be hurled against Russia and, in return, against the West, or against the West, and, in return, against Russia. We, in Britain, may have four minutes' notice that this is going to happen. It is hoped that, in America, there may be twenty-five minutes notice. And what shall we be having notice of? We shall be having notice that a very large proportion of our population will be killed outright, and that the remainder will die a slow and agonizing death. It is not expected by experts that anyone in Britain will survive.

So long as the present policy of 'instant retaliation' persists, there is a very grave danger that something which is not a Russian nuclear attack will be mistaken for such an attack. In this case, what our side believes to be retaliation will appear to the other side to be an unprovoked attack and full-scale nuclear war will begin. This has very nearly happened several times already. There is a powerful radar station at Thule in the north of Greenland which is intended to give warning of the approach of Soviet bombers. Pilots of planes containing H-bombs have been so thoroughly trained that they can be in the air within two minutes of receiving warning. Several times warning has been given when it turned out that what radar was showing was a flight of geese. Once, at least, the moon was mistaken for a Russian attack and only the accidental interposition of an iceberg which broke communications prevented a retaliatory attack. On all these occasions, the bombers started on the journey of destruction. Our Prime Minister has assured us that there will be no war by accident.* One must suppose that he has never heard of these incidents. A more realistic view is expressed in a report on disarmament by the United Nations Association in March 1961, which concludes (p. 19): 'We doubt whether there can be, in the long run, a world at all without disarmament. A spectre haunts us: a flock of wild geese flies silently across the white Arctic and into a Soviet or a U.S. radar warning screen. The screen represents the geese as missiles. The U.S. Government or the Soviet Union (as the case may be) – immediately mounts a retaliatory nuclear strike. The typhoon of nuclear war begins. The geese fly solemnly onwards, sole survivors of the last world war. This improbable picture is not quite impossible. It symbolizes at least the present extraordinary phoney peace, in all its unreason and inhumanity. The final irrationality of nuclear war demands a symbol. Let it be the geese which shall stand for it, a warning as clear as the cry of those other geese, so long ago, to the Romans on the Capitol.'

In addition to the chance of human error, there is always the chance of a mechanical fault. The mechanisms involved are very complex, and no one can be sure that after bombers have been started in error, the message recalling them will be duly received. If it is not, the human race perishes. Can anything justify the running of such a risk?

Nevertheless, the negotiators of the West, and also of the East, pursue their leisurely way considering – so we

* House of Commons, 29 November 1960.

must suppose – that the extermination of their population would be a smaller misfortune than some slight concession to the 'enemy'. This is the politics of Bedlam. If the negotiators on either side were sane men or less immersed than they are in detail, they would realize that a nuclear war, entailing these awful consequences, is far the greatest risk that is being incurred, and that a reasonable give and take leading to agreement is the only policy compatible with sanity or humane feeling or with reluctance to condemn ourselves, our children, our friends, and our nation to a totally futile death. Meanwhile, pride, love of power, and belief in the possibilities of unending bluff, blind the statesmen of East and West to their obvious duty to humanity and allow them to pursue their murderous game unchecked.

The spread of nuclear weapons to Powers which have not hitherto had them is universally admitted to increase very greatly the danger of a nuclear war. At first America was the only nuclear Power, then America and Russia, then America and Russia and Britain. The acquisition of nuclear weapons by France has probably occurred. There is reason to think that Israel will possess them before long and, if so, the United Arab Republic is sure to follow suit. It cannot be long before Communist China insists upon becoming a nuclear Power. Any two nuclear Powers may quarrel, and, if they do, the system of alliances will make a world war certain. The number of pairs of nuclear Powers that may quarrel increases much faster than the number of nuclear Powers. While only two Powers possessed nuclear weapons, there was only one such pair. While there are three nuclear Powers, there are three such pairs. With four Powers, the number rises to six; with five, to ten; with six, to fifteen; and so on. It is not only for this reason that the spread of H-bombs to new Powers is dangerous. It is also because there is an increase in the risk that some Government may be reckless or fanatical or mad. It is not so long since a Great Power was controlled by a madman, and there is no reason to think that a repetition of such an event is impossible or even improbable. To quote Seymour Melman once more: 'The analysis of technical feasibility of inspection for disarmament takes on special importance in view of the present or imminent availability of nuclear weapons to many nations. The means for the extermination of the human species thus pass into the hands of many Governments, large and small' (p. ix).

The suspension of tests is important on two quite different grounds. On the one hand, fall-out distributes radio-active poisons throughout the world. Some of these cause leukemia and cancer, while others affect the genital tract and lead to the birth of idiots or monsters. But there is another reason for the prohibition of tests, which is that without them a Power which has not yet possessed nuclear weapons cannot effectively manufacture them. After years of detailed negotiation, it had seemed that an agreement prohibiting tests was imminent, but at this point Khrushchev introduced his 'troika' proposal according to which the necessary inspections were to be carried out by three men, one Eastern, one Western, and one neutral. According to his suggestion, they were only to act when they were unanimous. It is not clear that he was prepared to insist upon unanimity, but his suggestion so angered the West that an agreement prohibiting tests became improbable. For the present, hope of an end to tests is almost extinguished by the Soviet decision to resume tests, with the inevitable American reaction.

The almost certain outcome is that in this, as in all other matters concerning disarmament, nothing whatever will be done in the near future in spite of the fact, which is universally recognized, that by doing nothing the Powers continually increase the risk of nuclear catastrophe.

Let us now pass from the dreary record of inaction to the consideration of what should be done if the human race is to have a chance of continued existence.

The first step should be the stopping of tests. Of this I have already spoken sufficiently. The next step should be the prevention of the spread of nuclear weapons to new countries. This could easily be achieved if the existing nuclear Powers were agreed upon it. There is no reason to think that it would have any effect upon the balance of power. The West would regret the acquisition of H-bombs by Communist China, and the East would regret their acquisition by France and Western Germany. But there is no way of securing that they shall spread only to one side, and no reason, therefore, to think that either side would lose by preventing their spread everywhere.

The next step, which would be much more difficult, would be a general agreement to cease the manufacture of nuclear weapons. This, of course, would require a very thorough system of inspection, but there is reason to believe that such a system could be effective and trustworthy. This is the conclusion arrived at in the book on *Inspection for Disarmament* already quoted above. I think, although this is not suggested in Melman's book, that it would be a good thing if there were neutrals among the inspectors, and if, in case of disagreement, the neutral inspectors were to make the report of their findings public.

In regard to inspection, there is a difficulty as to existing stocks. It would be very easy to conceal these, and hardly possible for an inspectorate to discover the concealment. There are, however, ways of circumventing this difficulty. An H-bomb is useless unless there are means of delivering it on enemy territory, and the necessary launching sites, so long as they are fixed, are easily detected. This would not apply to movable sites such as are afforded by Polaris submarines. But a submarine cannot easily be built in secret, and it should not be difficult to discover what submarines capable of carrying H-bombs have been built.

There is one possible reform which would be immensely useful if the nations could be persuaded to adopt it. That is the prohibition of foreign troops on any territory. I am afraid, however, that this is not likely to be achieved except by a system of general disarmament. American troops in Britain and Western Europe are considered essential by NATO (although not, apparently, by the best American authorities – see Kahn, *On Thermonuclear War*), and Russian troops in such countries as Hungary and Eastern Germany are obviously necessary if Russia is to keep the population of those countries in subjection. Nevertheless, as one of the more distant aims in the pursuit of peace, this measure is to be borne in mind as one to be achieved if and when it becomes practicable.

Khrushchev's proposal for complete and general disarmament should be taken far more seriously than it has been taken in the West. The West, as often before with Russian proposals, has maintained that the Soviet Government will not agree to adequate inspection. Khrushchev said, at first, that he would tolerate any degree of inspection *after* disarmament, but not before. He must have known that the West could not agree to this. If the West were to disarm and were to discover, too late, that the East had not disarmed, the discoveries revealed by inspection would no longer serve any useful purpose. But Khrushchev has also said that if universal and complete disarmament is decided upon, he will tolerate any degree of inspection as soon as agreement is reached. The West has been careful not to discover what precisely Khrushchev would accept in the way of inspection. It has been content to reject his proposal as something not intended seriously. This was a grievous error which would not have been committed if the West had genuinely desired disarmament. Instead of investigating Khrushchev's proposal, the Western Powers put forward proposals of their own and thereby kept alive indefinitely the futile contest of argument and counter-argument.

There is one other matter which is likely to be of very great importance within a decade. It is that of manned satellites in orbits round the earth. Such satellites would pass periodically over enemy territory and might drop bombs from a very great height. If they stayed at a considerable distance above the earth, they would be invulnerable, but the damage that they could do would be enormous. We must expect, if nothing is done to prevent such an appalling situation, that, before many years have passed, outer space will be full of these satellites raining death and destruction upon the countries beneath them. As yet, since this has not yet happened, it should be possible to prevent it. It should be possible to reach an agreement that the sending of missiles either into orbits round the earth or into remoter regions should be under

international control and should not be undertaken by
any single nation or group of nations. The difficulty at
present is that Russia appears to be more proficient than
the United States in this matter and that, therefore,
Russia's confidence and the United States' bruised pride
will be an obstacle to mutual understanding. We must
hope that before long there will be equality between
Russia and the United States in this matter. Russian
present superiority is to be regretted, not because it is
Russian, but because it is an obstacle to agreement. It
would be equally regrettable if the superiority were that
of the United States.

It is not only earth satellites that are to be expected
before the end of the present century. We must expect
that it will be possible to send men first to the moon and
then to Mars and Venus. To many, all this may still sound
fantastic, but it is being seriously considered by American military authorities, and presumably also by those of
the U.S.S.R. One eminent military authority on being confronted with the likelihood of Russians being the first to
reach the moon, solemnly argued that this would not
matter, since the United States would counter the Russian move by landing on Mars and Venus.* I think it is
important to bear in mind such possibilities of the near
future. The world in which we are now living would have
seemed, before 1945, too horrible to be endured, but, in

* Lt-General Donald L. Putt, Deputy Chief of Staff, U.S.
Air Force, giving evidence before a House Committee on Armed
Services, 25 February 1958, said: 'We should not regard control of the moon as the ultimate means of insuring peace among
earth nations.' This, he said, would be only 'a first step towards
stations on planets far more distant from which control over the
moon might then be exercised' (*I. F. Stone's Weekly*, 20 October
1958).

the course of sixteen years, we have got used to it. Probably, sixteen years hence, if we exist still, we shall look back to the world of 1961 as a happy and easy-going paradise in comparison to that we shall then be enduring.

And all for what? We must expect rival parties of Russian Commissars and American Marines to travel at enormous expense to the surface of the moon and to keep themselves alive there for a few days while they search for each other. When they find each other, they will exterminate each other. Each side will hear of the extermination of the other side and will proclaim a public holiday to celebrate the glorious victory. This is the kind of cosmically laughable tragedy towards which the statesmen of the world are leading us. Perhaps – just perhaps – as in imagination they soar above our atmosphere, some minute scrap of common sense or common humanity may find its way into their minds, and they may agree that our terrestrial quarrels should not be spread throughout the universe to display our folly and wickedness to whatever living beings happier planets may contain.

To conclude this somewhat gloomy chapter: we must become aware that the hatred, the expenditure of time and money and intellectual ability upon weapons of destruction, the fear of what we may do to each other, and the imminent daily and hourly risk of an end to all that man has achieved – we must be aware, I say, that all this is a product of human folly. It is not a decree of Fate. It is not something imposed by natural conditions. It is an evil springing from human minds, rooted in ancient cruelty and superstition, appropriate, perhaps, to savage hordes long ago, but, in our age, destructive, first, of happiness and, then, in all likelihood, of life. One thing only is needed to turn this Hell into a Heaven: it is that East and West, alike, should cease to hate and fear each other and should become aware of the common happiness that they can enjoy if they are willing to work together. It is in our hearts that the evil lies, and it is from our hearts that it must be plucked out.

10 *Territorial Problems*

THERE are a number of territorial questions which will
have to be decided before peace can be considered secure.
Formosa, Korea, and Laos are among the most obvious.
It is not easy to think of any principle for deciding such
questions which would be acceptable to both sides. The
West is apt to maintain that it would accept the principle
of self-determination, but, on a closer scrutiny, it appears
that the West is only willing to apply this principle to
countries which are, at present, in the Soviet orbit. It is
not ready to insist upon democratic self-determination
in Spain or Portugal, and it is doubtful whether it would
accept the principle in those parts of the Western hemisphere where there might prove to be a pro-Communist
majority. It is quite impossible at present to foresee the
outcome of negotiations designed to settle such questions.
The only thing that can be said quite positively is that
they should be settled by negotiation and not by mutual
threats in the manner of Brinkmanship, but by com-
promises in which neutrals should be invited to par-
ticipate.

The West has been to blame, ever since the Russian
Revolution, for a Rip van Winkle policy. For a long
time, the West refused to acknowledge the Soviet
Government. America and UNO are still refusing to
acknowledge the Communist Government of China. The
West has not acknowledged the Government of Eastern
Germany, or recognized the definitive character of the
Oder–Neisse frontier. As regards this last, the West Ger-
man Government and the vast majority of individual

Germans everywhere passionately resent it, but the difficulties of any revision in this respect are quite insuperable. In the first place, the Communist bloc will never consent, except as a result of defeat in war. But such defeat would only happen in an all-out nuclear war in which the West would be equally defeated and probably all ordered government would come to an end. In the second place, the restoration of Germany's former frontiers would entail a repetition in reverse order of the appalling large-scale cruelties which were practised by Russians and Poles when the German population was expelled from the regions that were no longer legally German.

Recognition of an existing régime should not be regarded as implying approval. It should be regarded merely as an acknowledgement of existing facts. The West, in the end, came to admit this as regards the U.S.S.R., but it did not learn from this experience the unwisdom of tardiness in acknowledging régimes which cannot be upset without world war.

Much the most difficult and dangerous territorial problem facing the world at the present time is that of Germany and Berlin. This question is, at present, in a state of such acute crisis that anything said about it may well be obsolete before it can be printed. Nevertheless, something must be said about how it should be treated and about how it should *not* be treated. It should not be treated by sabre-rattling on both sides, which, unfortunately, is being practised. For example, in February 1961, Admiral Burke, the United States Chief of Naval Operations, said: 'I personally do not think there is going to be a general war as long as we retain our ability to destroy the Soviet Union no matter what she does. We

now have that capability (*The Times,* 17 February 1961).
Mr Khrushchev made a very similar speech on 9 July
1961, saying: 'Any aggressor, should he raise his hand
against the Soviet Union or its friends, should receive
worthy rebuff. The Soviet army have at their disposal the
necessary quantity of thermonuclear weapons; the most
perfect means of delivery – close and medium range
rockets and inter-continental rockets. May those who
are thinking about war not think that they will be saved
by distance. No, if the imperialists start a war, it will end
with the complete defeat of imperialism. Mankind will
once and for all put an end to a system which gives rise
to predatory wars' (*The Times,* 10 July 1961). I agree
with Admiral Burke and Mr Khrushchev that forces on
their own sides will be capable of exterminating the
enemy, but each of these eminent philanthropists has
failed to notice that the enemy will also be able to exterminate his side. These mutual threats contribute
nothing whatever towards a settlement, and only serve
to make war more probable. The immediate question at
issue is West Berlin, and it must be clear to all parties
that, in a war, practically all the inhabitants of West
Berlin would perish. On the face of it, this is not a very
effective way of protecting them.

The question of West Berlin is exceedingly complex
and it may be well to review the rights and wrongs briefly.

Owing to the policy of unconditional surrender, which
was adopted against Germany in the Second World War,
the war did not end with a peace treaty, but with an
agreement among the victors as to how Germany should
be governed. Germany was divided into four zones:
American, British, French, and Russian, each to be ad-
ministered by the Power to whom the zone was assigned.

Berlin, which was entirely surrounded by the Russian zone, was similarly divided into four sectors in each of which the Power concerned was to be omnipotent. But, by an almost incredible folly, the West made no provision for freedom to come and go, to or from, its sectors over the Russian zone. The Russians took advantage of this omission when they imposed the blockade in 1948. When the air-lift proved that the blockade was futile, the Russians consented to an agreement admitting freedom of ingress and egress to and from West Berlin. The three Western zones of Germany had, meantime, been united and permitted to establish democratic self-government. The same thing had been done with the three Western sectors of Berlin. All negotiations as regards Germany or Berlin depended for their legal validity upon the agreements reached at Yalta and Potsdam. These agreements were intended to be temporary until such time as a peace treaty with Germany could be concluded. The division of Germany betwen East and West has hitherto made such a treaty impossible. The Soviet Government has now announced that it will conclude a treaty with East Germany which will put an end to the wartime agreement between Russia and the West, and will, therefore, abolish the legal status of West Berlin unless this is acknowledged by a fresh treaty with East Germany by the West. The West considers that there is no reason to expect East Germany to be willing to conclude such a treaty, and the Soviet Government has announced that it will not bring pressure to bear upon East Germany with the view to the conclusion of such a treaty.

It must be understood that the question of substance in the whole issue is the right of free communications between West Berlin and West Germany without which

West Berlin would be completely at the mercy of East Germany. Since East Germany is completely subject to the Soviet Government, this would mean that West Berlin could only survive by completely submitting to whatever terms the Soviet Government might choose to exact.

Legally, the position of the West is impregnable. The rights of the West in relation to West Berlin rest on an agreement between the U.S., Britain, France, and U.S.S.R., which cannot legally be abrogated unilaterally and which subsists until there is a general peace treaty, either with Germany as a whole, or with each of its two parts. Khrushchev demands the conclusion of such a treaty, but announces that, if the West is obdurate, the U.S.S.R will itself conclude a treaty with East Germany, and will consider that thereby the rights of the West in relation to West Berlin have been terminated. This view is legally indefensible.

Morally, Khrushchev is infringing what both sides must accept as an absolute rule if nuclear war is to be avoided, since he is demanding, by the threat of war, a change in the *status quo* immensely advantageous to the East and immensely disadvantageous to the West. Granted that nuclear war is, for both sides, the worst disaster that could possibly happen, it follows that any change in the *status quo* must be by negotiation, not by the threat of force, and that it must not seriously alter the balance of power, since, if it does, it will not be agreed to. It may be argued that, since nuclear war is the worst thing possible, if one side threatens it, the other side should give way. But, rightly or wrongly, nations will not behave in such a manner. National pride combined with the belief that one's cause is righteous, will inevitably lead to threats being met by counter-threats. It is this that makes the policy of Brinkmanship so dangerous. At the moment, both sides are engaged in this policy and, in the question of Berlin, the chief blame of this appallingly dangerous situation lies with the U.S.S.R.

The motives which have led to the Russian desire to make life painful for the inhabitants of West Berlin have not been openly stated, but are, in fact, fairly clear. East Germany and East Berlin are poor and their Governments are hated by a large majority of the population. West Germany and West Berlin are prosperous and their Governments are popular. A large number of the inhabitants of East Germany escaped to the West, which they could only do so long as West Berlin was accessible to them and communications between West Berlin and West Germany were open. This situation is humiliating to the Communist world. The only remedy, from the Communist point of view, is to make West Berlin as poor and miserable as East Berlin, and to close the escape-route from West Berlin to West Germany. This is not a purpose which any humane person can applaud.

It cannot be said, however, that the West has dealt as wisely as it might with the Berlin crisis. If the status of West Berlin could be guaranteed, there would be no good reason against acknowledgement of the East German Government by the West. The West ought to take steps to find out whether the East German Government would be willing to preserve the status of West Berlin and the freedom of its communications with the outer world in return for the recognition of the East German Government by the Western Powers. So far as has appeared, hitherto, the West does not know what are the intentions of the East German Government in this respect. It is certainly not worth while to prolong the crisis and risk a general war if the status of West Berlin can be preserved. The West ought to be taking immediate steps to find out whether a treaty with Eastern Germany, involving, on our side, recognition and, on the other side, a guarantee not to change the status of West Berlin, can be concluded. There has been talk of making the whole of Berlin into what is called a 'free city', but it has never been made clear whether this would entail free communication with the West. If it would, the proposal would deserve support. As regards free communication, it is important that West Berlin should retain its present airport at Tempelhof, and it is ominous that East Germany is demanding its abandonment. It was possession of the airport at Tempelhof that enabled West Berlin to survive the blockade.

From the Western point of view the difficulty of the situation arises from the impossibility of any local defence of West Berlin. The whole surrounding territory is open to Russian troops, and the only effective resistance possible to the West is an all-out nuclear war. In such a war, it is to be expected that all the inhabitants of Berlin, both East and West, would perish – a curious result of 'protection'. Protection, in fact, so long as Russia is persistent, can consist only in the threat of nuclear war without its actually taking place. If the threat is thought to be only bluff, it accords no protection. If it is thought to be bluff, but is not, the human race perishes.

Possibly, the West might undertake to submit the Berlin question to arbitration and rally the whole non-Communist world against the threat of war by the Powers which facetiously call themselves 'the peace-loving nations'. Mr Dean Rusk has recently made a not wholly dissimilar suggestion. But it is doubtful whether either side would agree to such a proposal.

It is not only Berlin, but the whole status of Germany, which makes the approach to a stable peace very difficult. Almost every German naturally desires the restoration of a united Germany. While part of Germany is Communist, and part non-Communist, it is not easy to see how this can be achieved. It is to be noted that Khrushchev has lately revived the Rapacki Plan, according to which the whole of Germany, and also some countries to the East of it, should be disarmed and neutralized and protected by a guarantee to which both Russia and the West should subscribe. From the point of view of world peace, this is a wholly admirable suggestion, and it is much to be wished that the Western Powers would take it up, but I am afraid that there is little hope of their doing so. It is vehemently opposed by Adenauer, who wants a strong military Germany. It is also opposed by America, Britain, and France, who want German armed assistance in resisting Russia. Nobody in the West seems to have noticed that the Rapacki Plan involves the disarmament of several Communist Powers, which would be an adequate counterpoise to the disarmament of Western Germany.

The reliance on Western Germany by the Western Powers has dangerous aspects which are carefully ignored. German troops are still commanded by Generals many of whom are ex-Nazis. German revival under Hitler might well be a precedent. There are German troops stationed in Britain at the invitation of the British Government. It is surprising that what we all felt in 1940 can be so quickly forgotten.

All these tangled problems would become immeasurably easier to solve if the world were to adopt Khrushchev's proposal of general and complete disarmament, which, throughout the present crisis, he has frequently renewed. What makes the Rapacki Plan unacceptable to Germans is the fact that under it Germany and no other Great Power would be disarmed. If disarmament were general, this objection would lose its force.

In the problem of Germany and Berlin, none of the Great Powers of East and West have, so far, emerged with credit, or shown any degree of wise statesmanship. Perhaps, as the threat of nuclear war grows more imminent, both sides may withdraw from the brink and find some way by which their populations may be allowed to remain in existence. But it seems at least equally likely that nationalist pride and determination not to yield to threats will drive both sides on until both perish in mutual folly.

11 *A Stable World*

I AM writing at a dark moment (July 1961), and it is impossible to know whether the human race will last long enough for what I write to be published, or, if published, to be read. But as yet hope is possible, and while hope is possible, despair is a coward's part.

The most important question before the world at the present time is this: is it possible to achieve anything that any one desires by means of war? Kennedy and Khrushchev say *yes*; sane men say *no*. On this supreme question Kennedy and Khrushchev are at one. If one could suppose them both capable of a rational estimate of probabilities, we should have to believe that both agree that the time has come for Man to become extinct. But, of course, this is not what they are both thinking. Pride, arrogance, fear of loss of face, and ideological intolerance have obscured their power of judgement. Their own blindness is reinforced by a similar blindness on the part of powerful pressure groups, and by a popular hysteria generated by their own propaganda and that of their colleagues and subordinates.

What, in these circumstances, can be done to counteract the turbulent follies of powerful men?

A pessimist might argue: why seek to preserve the human species? Should we not rather rejoice in the prospect of an end to the immense load of suffering and hate and fear which has hitherto darkened the life of Man? Should we not contemplate with rejoicing a new future for our planet, peaceful at last, sleeping quietly at last after coming to the end of the long nightmare of pain and horror?

To any student of history contemplating the dreadful record of folly and cruelty and misery that has constituted most of human life hitherto, such questions must come in moments of imaginative sympathy. Perhaps our survey may tempt us to acquiesce in an end, however tragic and however final, to a species so incapable of joy.

But the pessimist has only half of the truth, and to my mind the less important half. Man has not only the correlative capacities for cruelty and suffering, but also potentialities of greatness and splendour, realized, as yet, very partially, but showing what life might be in a freer and happier world. If Man will allow himself to grow to his full stature, what he may achieve is beyond our present capacity to imagine. Poverty, illness, and loneliness could become rare misfortunes. Reasonable expectation of happiness could dispel the night of fear in which too many now wander lost. And with the progress of evolution, what is now the shining genius of an eminent few might become a common possession of the many. All this is possible, indeed probable, in the thousands of centuries that lie before us, if we do not rashly and madly destroy ourselves before we have reached the maturity that should be our goal. No, let us not listen to the pessimist, for, if we do, we are traitors to Man's future.

Leaving these distant hopes, what must be done in our own age?

First of all, we must get rid of war. At the present time, the nations engaged in the cold war spend on preparations for slaughter thirty thousand million pounds a year, or five hundred and seventy thousand pounds a minute. Consider what this expenditure might do to promote human welfare. More than half the population of the world is under-nourished, not because it need be, but because the richer nations prefer killing each other to keeping the poorer nations alive and helping them to achieve a higher standard of life. Nothing, while our present mentality persists, induces the richer nations to help the others except the hope of buying their support in the cold war. Why should we not, instead, use our wealth to buy their support for secure peace?

There is a fear, fostered by those who are interested in the armament industry, whether as employers or as workers, that disarmament might cause a disastrous economic dislocation. This fear is not shared by those who are best qualified to pronounce as to its validity. I will refer the reader to two very competent and careful discussions, one in *The Nation's Business* (the organ of the U.S. Chamber of Commerce) for October 1959, the other by Senator Hubert H. Humphrey (Chairman of the U.S. Senate Sub-Committee on Disarmament) in *Think* for January 1960. Both these entirely orthodox authorities are agreed that experience at the end of the Second World War showed the possibility of a smooth transition from a war economy to a peace economy, given certain obvious and entirely practicable precautions. I think, therefore, that we may dismiss the paradoxical theory that we can only keep alive by preparing to kill each other.

If a World Government is to work smoothly, certain economic conditions will have to be fulfilled. One of these, which is beginning to receive widespread recognition, is the raising of the standard of life in what are now under-developed countries to the level which prevails among the most prosperous populations of the West. Until a certain economic equality among the different parts of the world has been achieved, the poorer nations will envy the richer ones, and the richer ones will dread violent action on the part of those who are less prosperous.

But this is not the most difficult economic measure that may be necessary. Various raw materials are essential to industry. Of these, at present, oil is one of the most important. Probably uranium, though no longer needed for purposes of war, will be essential for the industrial use of nuclear energy. There is no justice in the private ownership of such essential raw materials – and I think we must include in undesirable private ownership, not only that by individuals or companies, but also that by separate States. The raw materials without which industry is impossible should belong to the International Authority and be granted to separate nations in accordance with the two principles of justice and aptitude for their use. Nations which are lacking in this aptitude should be helped to acquire it.

In a stable world such as we are envisaging, there could be in many ways a great deal more freedom than there is at present. There would, however, be some new limitations on freedom, since it would be necessary to inculcate loyalty to the International Government and to curb incitements to war by single nations or groups of nations. Subject to this limitation, there should be freedom of the Press, freedom of speech, and freedom of travel. There should be a very radical change in education. The young should no longer be taught to over-emphasize the merits of their own countries, to feel pride in those of their compatriots who had shown most skill in killing foreigners, or to adopt Mr Podsnap's maxim: 'Foreign nations, I am sorry to say, do as they do do.' History should be taught from an international point of view with little emphasis on wars and much emphasis upon peaceful achievements, whether in knowledge or art, or in exploration or adventure. The education authorities of a single country should not be permitted by the International Government to stir up chauvinist feeling or to advocate armed rebellion against the International Government. Apart from these limitations, there should be a much greater freedom in education than there is at present. Unpopular opinions, unless they were such as to cause a danger of war, should be tolerated in teachers. The whole emphasis, in all teaching of history or social subjects, should be on Man and not on separate nations or groups of nations.

Both individuals and groups have two opposite kinds of incentive: one is cooperation, and the other is competition. Every advance of scientific technique increases the desirable sphere of cooperation and diminishes the desirable sphere of competition. I do not mean that competition should disappear altogether as an incentive, but I do mean that it should not take such forms as inflicting widespread injury, more particularly, of course, in the shape of war. It should be one of the aims of education to make young people aware of the possibilities of worldwide cooperation and to generate the habit of thinking about the interests of mankind as a whole. As a result of such teaching, there should be a general growth of friendly feeling, and a diminution of the propaganda of hate which has hitherto formed part of State education in most countries.

There are those who feel that a world without war would be a dull world. It must be admitted that, in the world as it is now, many people lead very uninteresting and circumscribed lives, and some among them feel that at least they are able to do something of importance and find relief from boredom and monotony when, in the course of a war, they are transported to distant countries and have a chance to see ways of life other than that to which they were accustomed at home. I think that provision should be made for adventure, and even dangerous adventure, in the lives of such of the young as desire it. Such adventure, which would normally be cooperative, would demand discipline, cooperation, and responsibility, and even obedience, without which the necessary toughening of fibre might be lacking and which now form the basis of many people's love of war. There should be opportunity to join scientific expeditions for the exploration of the Arctic and the Antarctic, the Himalayas and the Andes. And for those who crave something even more adventurous, there should be space-travel, which is on the verge of becoming possible. With the weight of armaments removed, it would be possible to provide at the public expense all that the restless young could desire in ways not, as at present, causing misery and disaster and a risk of the end of Man.

If the danger of war were removed, there would be a transition period during which men's thoughts and emotions were still moulded by the turbulent past. During this transition period, the full benefit to be expected from the ending of war could not be realized. There would still be an excess of competitive feeling, and the older generation, at least, would not readily adapt their minds to the new world that would be in process of being created. While the work of reorientation was going on, there would be need of an effort, possibly involving some limitation of freedom, to bring about the necessary adaptation.

I do not think, however, that this adaptation would prove impossible. Human nature is at least nine-tenths nurture, and only the remaining tenth is genetic. The part which is due to nurture can be dealt with by education. Probably, in time, even the part that is genetic will prove amenable to science. Let us suppose that the transition period has been successfully traversed, and ask ourselves what sort of a world might be hoped for as a result.

How would art and literature and science fare in such a world? I think we may hope that liberation from the load of fear, private economic fear and public fear of war, would cause the human spirit to soar to hitherto undreamt of heights. Men, hitherto, have always been cramped in their hopes and aspirations and imagination by the limitations of what has been possible. They have sought relief from pain and sorrow in the hope of an after-life in Heaven. As the Negro spiritual says, 'I'm going to tell God all of my troubles, when I go home.' But there is no need to wait for Heaven. There is no reason why life on earth should not be filled with happiness. There is no reason why imagination should have to take refuge in myth. In such a world as men could now make, if they chose, it could be freely creative within the framework of our terrestrial existence. In recent times, knowledge has grown so fast that its acquisition has been confined to a tiny minority of experts, few of whom have had the energy or the capacity to impregnate it with poetic feeling and cosmic insight. The Ptolemaic System of astronomy found its best poetic expression in Dante, and for this it had to wait some fifteen hundred years. We are suffering from undigested science. But in a world of more adventurous education this undigested mass would be assimilated and our poetry and art could be enlarged

a) cf G. M. Carstairs: This Island Now, 1962, pp 304,83 on 'determinism' & personal responsibility, according to Trend+oden — see also Gabor, Inventing the future, p. 127

to embrace new worlds to be depicted in new epics. The liberation of the human spirit may be expected to lead to new splendours, new beauties and new sublimities impossible in the cramped and fierce world of the past. If our present troubles can be conquered, Man can look forward to a future immeasurably longer than his past, inspired by a new breadth of vision, a continuing hope perpetually fed by a continuing achievement. Man has made a beginning creditable for an infant – for, in a biological sense, Man, the latest of species, is still an infant. No limit can be set to what he may achieve in the future. I see, in my mind's eye, a world of glory and joy, a world where minds expand, where hope remains undimmed, and what is noble is no longer condemned as treachery to this or that paltry aim. All this can happen if we will let it happen. It rests with our generation to decide between this vision and an end decreed by folly.

Recommended Books

Assault at Arms, a Policy for Disarmament, General Sir Ronald Adam, Bt, G.C.B., D.S.O. and Charles Judd, C.B.E. (U.N.A. of Great Britain and Northern Ireland, London, 1960).

Brighter Than a Thousand Suns: The Moral and Political History of the Atomic Scientists, Robert Jungk (Gollancz, London, 1958, and Penguin Books, 1960).

Can We End the Cold War? A Study in American Foreign Policy, Leo Perla (Macmillan, New York, 1960).

Community of Fear, Harrison Brown and James Real (Center for the Study of Democratic Institutions, Santa Barbara, California, 1960).

Disarmament, the Intensified Effort (1955–8) (Department of State, Washington, D.C., July 1958).

Fallout, A Study of Superbombs, Strontium 90 and Survival, ed. John M. Fowler (Basic Books, New York, 1960).

Inspection for Disarmament, ed. Seymour Melman (Columbia University Press, New York, 1958).

1970 Without Arms Control, National Planning Association (Washington, D.C., 1958).

No Carte Blanche to Capricorn: The Folly of Nuclear War Strategy, Édouard le Ghait (Brookfield House, New York, 1960).

No More War, Linus Pauling (Dodd Mead & Co., New York, 1958).

Nuclear Explosions and Their Effects, second edition (Publications Division, Ministry of Information and Broadcasting, Delhi, 1958).

On Thermonuclear War, Herman Kahn (Princeton University Press, Princeton, 1960).

Peacemaker or Powder-Monkey: Canada's Role in a Revolutionary World, James M. Minifie (McClelland and Stewart, Canada, 1960).

Survival, Vol. II, No. 2, and Vol. III, No. 1 (Institute for Strategic Studies, London, 1960 and 1961).

The Arms Race, A Programme for World Disarmament, Philip Noel-Baker (Stevens and Sons, London, 1958).

The Causes of World War Three, C. Wright Mills (Simon and Schuster, New York, 1958).

The Logic of Defence, a Short Study of the 'Nuclear' Dilemma, Lt-Col. Patrick Lort-Phillips, D.S.O. (Radical Publications, England, 1959).

Towards Sanity; A Study of the Defence of Britain, Lt-Col. Patrick Lort-Phillips, D.S.O. (Radical Publications, Wales, 1960).

Why We Are Here, H. L. Keenleyside (National Committee for Control of Radiation Hazards, Montreal, 1960).